ABITA | COOKING
BEER® | LOUISIANA TRUE

ABITA BREWING COMPANY, LLC
ABITA SPRINGS, LA

CREDITS

Library of Congress Cataloging-in-Publication Data available.

ISBN 978-0-615-23864-7

Printed in Singapore.

Project Coordination, Copywriting & Design by
Innovative Advertising

Principle Photography by
Jackson Hill & Southern Lights Photography

Food Styling by
Angie Mosier

Cooking by
Chef Matt Hooks

Editing by
Barbara Gibbs Ostmann

Historic Photography provided by
Mary Lou Eichorn & Sally Stassi at the
Williams Research Center: Historic New Orleans Collection &
Earl K. Long Library at the University of New Orleans

Abita Brewing Company, LLC
P.O. Box 1510
Abita Springs, LA 70420

www.abita.com

DEDICATIONS

This book is dedicated to the customers of Abita Beer. Thank you for supporting our promise to put quality before quantity and for always staying "Louisiana True". We commit to honor your dedication by always creating full-flavored, all natural brews that are the best of any beer in the world.

TABLE OF CONTENTS

FOREWORD BY CHEF SUSAN SPICER 1

PREFACE 3

ACKNOWLEDGMENTS 5

MARCELLE BIENVENU 7

HISTORY OF CRAFT BREWING 9

HISTORY OF ABITA BEER 11

HISTORY OF BEER IN NEW ORLEANS 15

THE PROCESS OF MAKING BEER 22

HOW TO ENJOY BEER 31

RECIPES 51

HOW TO COOK WITH ABITA BEER 53

STARTERS 55

    ceviche beer shots 57

    abita turbodog barbecued alligator legs 58

    golden abita pomodori with fresh crab fingers 59

    drunken mussels 61

    abita beer-battered tempura soft-shell crabs with ponzu dipping sauce 62

    cheddar & abita amber soup 66

oyster soup provencal 67

abita black-eyed pea vinaigrette salad 69

baby lettuces with purple haze raspberry balsamic vinaigrette 71

abita wild rice & cheese soup 72

abita beer bread 73

abita beer biscuits 75

wood grilled shrimp with louisiana strawberry salad &

abita strawberry lager vinaigrette 77

abita beer batter seafood beignets with sauce americaine 78

abita brew pub crab fingers 79

frank's fantastic easy-to-bake beer bread 81

beer hushpuppies 82

abita purple haze barbecue sauce 83

SEAFOOD 85

sauteed snapper with pecan meuniere accompanied by marcelle's rice pilaf 86

new orleans barbecue shrimp shortcakes with abita amber cream 90

nola's shrimp and smoked cheddar grits with abita beer-b-q glaze 93

bacco crab cakes with turbodog creole mustard aioli 97

delta's louisiana barbecue shrimp with abita golden 99

blackened redfish with abita amber braised cabbage & barbecued oysters 100

barbecue shrimp, abita style 102

susan spicer's crayfish curry 103

MAINS 105

really good gumbo 107

abita amber pulled pork 109

andouille sausage 110

turbodog cochon de lait 111

restoration ale wild mushroom & goat cheese tart 113

turbodog short ribs 115

abita amber marinated steak 116

abita pot roast 117

football brats with abita beer 119

poppy tooker's chicken etouffee 121

poppy tooker's creole carbonnades 122

deep-fried beer-braised short ribs po'boy 123

arroz con pollo y abita golden 125

abita amber beer jerk chicken 127

abita braised duck with cilantro rice 129

turbodog braised oxtails 130

grilled margarita pizza 133

beer-braised rabbit 136

shepherd's pie 137

abita pan-roasted chicken 138

abita root beer glazed pork tenderloin with tasso-cabbage hash 139

jockamo i.p.a. slow braised pork meat pie with spicy onion marmalade 140

SIDES 143

bernard's southern cooked greens 144

baked beans abita root beer style 145

warm potato salad with abita amber dressing 147

tempura fried vegetables 148

abita beer-braised greens 149

turbodog braised cabbage 150

ideas for vegetables 151

DESSERTS 153

louisiana true beeramisu 155

turbodog ice cream 157

abita purple haze bars 158

abita golden bananas 159

purple haze sorbet 161

root beer float with pirouette cookies 163

pecan spice beer cake with brown butter pecan glaze 164

INDEX 166

TABLE OF EQUIVALENTS & FOOD HANDLING 173

ABITA
BREWING COMPANY

ABITA
BEER ®

FOREWORD
BY CHEF SUSAN SPICER

When I was first invited to write the foreword to this cookbook it caused me to think about my experiences with Abita Beer in the past. Although some of them include cooking with this fine Louisiana product, more than a few of the memories involve holding a cold Abita in my hand while loud music and the laughter of friends play in the background. Both sorts evoke thoughts of home and good times.

I guess that's part of what makes Abita a perfect beer for cooking. If you live in the southeast, Abita Beer is a part of your life. You enjoy it with friends, you serve it with food and you use it in your recipes. The Abita Brewing Company goes out of their way to use locally grown ingredients whenever possible — something that's always important to me.

This book is a collection of recipes from some of the finest chefs in the New Orleans area and around the United States. I'm always amazed that wherever I travel I can find Abita Beer these days...a welcome friend when you're far from home. Some of the chefs in this cookbook don't own restaurants. They're people who cook for their friends, make dinner every night and just love creating good food. If they are your friends, they've probably already shared these recipes with you. That attracted me to this cookbook too — good food is all about sharing.

I learned when I wrote my first cookbook that some people who buy them never intend to try a single recipe — they just love to read and learn. For those people, this cookbook is a good choice. You'll find out about the history of beer, how to enjoy beer and how to use beer in your everyday cooking. Perhaps you'll even get inspired and try a recipe or two. You won't be sorry.

I'm pleased to introduce you to *Abita Beer, Cooking Louisiana True.* I hope it will create some wonderful memories for you too.

Chef Susan Spicer has played an integral role in the New Orleans culinary scene for more than 25 years. A recipient of the James Beard Award for Best Chef, Southeast Region, and chosen for the Mondavi Culinary Excellence Award, her restaurant Bayona is one of the Crescent City's most highly regarded. Her leadership in the local culinary scene has helped bring women to the forefront of cooking globally.

PREFACE

When people learn that you work for Abita Beer, they can't wait to tell you about their experiences with our product. As you might expect, over the years we've heard some great stories. How they desperately searched for their favorite Abita after a forced relocation by Hurricane Katrina. How their entire dorm room at LSU was decorated with an Abita Beer theme. Of course, there are some pretty funny stories that are not suitable for a family-oriented cookbook. Over and over, people talk to us about their experiences with Abita Beer and food. They want to share their favorite recipe using Turbodog or Amber. We learn about amazing meals they have enjoyed in restaurants all across the country that used Abita Beer as an ingredient or special menus where each course is paired with a different Abita Beer.

Since so many of you have shared your recipes with us, it seemed about time to share some of this knowledge with the rest of the world. In this cookbook we've assembled recipes from some of Louisiana's greatest chefs and restaurants. You'll also find selections from restaurants across the country — because Abita Beer is sold and enjoyed in more than 39 states. We've included recipe favorites from Abita Beer lovers from around the USA. Each recipe has been tested and tasted. We've tried to keep the book fun, but also full of valuable information about how beer is made, the history of brewing in Louisiana, and how to best enjoy Abita Beer with food.

We take great pride in creating all natural full-flavored ales and lagers at Abita Beer. It is rewarding to know that the care we have taken over the years to create a product line with a full range of flavors has inspired others to create wonderful meals using our product. In all that we do at the Abita Brewing Company, we make sure our product represents the best Louisiana has to offer. That's why we named the book *Abita Beer, Cooking Louisiana True.*

Thank you for your support of Abita Beer through the years. We hope you'll continue to tell us your Abita Beer stories and we look forward to hearing your experiences with the cookbook.

Cheers!

David Blossman

David Blossman
President
Abita Brewing Company
Abita Springs, Louisiana

ACKNOWLEDGMENTS

Cheers to the loyal Abita Beer drinkers everywhere. You inspire us everyday to create the finest and freshest ales and lagers. With your support we've grown from a small local brewery in the corner of what is now the Abita Brew Pub to the largest craft brewery in the Southeast. Thank you for your loyalty to the brand, attendance at Pub Crawls, Beer Dinners and so much more. Because of you, we'll always stay Louisiana True.

Many thanks to the "people who think" at Innovative Advertising for being the creative force behind the words and images in this project. Throughout the years the creative team at Innovative has helped us develop our brand and create the award-winning messages that define the Abita Brewing Company.

We appreciate the assistance of Mary Lou Eichorn and Sally Stassi at the Williams Research Center: Historic New Orleans Collection and the librarians at the Earl K. Long Library at the University of New Orleans for helping us discover the historical details and images that are seen in this book.

A special thank you to all the Louisiana chefs who have contributed to this book. Good food and fine dining are the backbone of tourism and culture in Louisiana. We appreciate your time, patience and dedication to Abita Beer. To all the chefs across the nation who contributed to this cookbook — thank you for sharing Abita Beer and helping to create loyal fans everywhere.

Thank you to the everyday heroes and Abita Beer drinkers who contributed their recipes to this book. We're so glad you included Abita in your recipes, and shared them with friends, family and everyone who reads this cookbook.

Thank you to Jackson Hill and Southern Lights Photography for the beautiful images in the book. We appreciate Food Stylist Angie Mosier and Chef Matt Hooks for working hard to make every dish look and taste delicious. Special thanks to cookbook editor Barbara Gibbs Ostmann who literally wrote the book on writing your own cookbook.

Merci beaucoup to Marcelle Bienvenu for cooking, checking and testing each and every recipe in this book and providing interesting content. Your wealth of knowledge and experience has added so much to this cookbook. When it comes to cooking, you are Louisiana True.

And finally, special thanks to the crew at the Abita Brewing Company; we couldn't do it without you.

MARCELLE BIENVENU

Marcelle Bienvenu was born in St. Martinville, a small town in southwestern Louisiana. St. Martinville is also the setting of Evangeline, Longfellow's legendary poem about early Acadian star-crossed lovers, Gabriel and Evangeline.

The Bienvenu family owned and published the Teche News, a wonderful foundation for a budding journalist. After graduation in 1967 from the University of Southwestern Louisiana, now University of Louisiana — Lafayette, Marcelle was hired as a feature writer for The Times-Picayune. In 1971, Time-Life Books beckoned and Marcelle left The Times-Picayune to work as a researcher and consultant on the books, *Foods of The World: American Cooking, Creole and Acadian,* and *The American Wilderness: The Bayous.*

Ms. Bienvenu has been featured in Food and Wine, Southern Living, Redbook, The New York Times, and Saveur, as well as in many local and regional publications. Since 1984, Marcelle has written a weekly food column, "Cooking Creole," for The Times-Picayune and contributes regularly to Louisiana Cookin' and Louisiana Life magazines.

In addition to her published articles in newspapers and magazines, Marcelle edited the Picayune's 1987 edition of *Creole Cook Book*, which was originally published in 1901, and reissued to celebrate the newspaper's 150th anniversary.

In 1991, Marcelle published her own cookbook, filled with recipes for the delicious cuisine of her native locale, *Who's Your Mama, Are You Catholic, and Can You Make a Roux?* A sequel of the same name was published in 1998. The first book has been recently republished after much demand for the out-of-print book. She is also the author of *Cajun*

Cooking for Beginners, published by Acadian House Publishing.

Marcelle has co-authored several books, including:
• *Eula Mae's Cajun Kitchen*, with Eula Mae Dore, published in 2002 by Harvard Common Press

• *Stir The Pot: The History of Cajun Cuisine*, with Carl and Ryan Brasseaux, published by Hippocrene in September 2005

Emeril Lagasse and Marcelle co-authored *Louisiana - Real & Rustic, Emeril's Creole Christmas, Emeril's TV Dinners, and Every Day's A Party*, published by William Morrow and Company, all of which were on The New York Times bestseller list. She also lent her talents to *Emeril Primetime, From Emeril's Kitchens, Emeril's Potluck, and Emeril's Delmonico: A Restaurant With a Past.*

Ms. Bienvenu has worked in public relations and as catering director and consultant for several restaurants, including Commander's Palace and K-Paul's Louisiana Kitchen in New Orleans, and Brennan's of Houston. From 1981-1984, she operated her own restaurant, Chez Marcelle, near Lafayette, Louisiana.

Bienvenu is French for "Welcome," or "Good to see you," and "Would you like some gumbo?" — an apt moniker for someone who has spent her life welcoming folks worldwide to taste the simple, yet delicious food she has known since birth. Close to her roots, Marcelle lives on Bayou Teche in St. Martinville, Louisiana, with her husband, Rock Lasserre.

Hops are the flowers of the hop vine and essential to the beer making process.

HISTORY OF CRAFT BREWING

The 1970s were a time of polyester pants, lava lamps, Day-Glo colors and light, low-calorie lager beers. The distinctive beer traditions and styles that immigrants from all over the world had brought to America were disappearing. Mass marketing and brewing industry consolidation reduced beer drinkers' choices to a flavorless few.

Beer lovers who wanted to enjoy unique brews that were outside of the mainstream began experimenting with home brewing. Soon these enthusiasts were inspired to start their own small brewing companies and share their tasty hobby with others. Their goal was to reintroduce the public to full-flavored beer and old-world traditions. By the 1980s, these microbrewing pioneers were blending European traditions with American ingenuity to create the foundations of the craft brewing industry.

The Brewers Association defines craft brewers with three key attributes. They must be small, with annual production of beer less than 2 million barrels. Craft brewers must be independent, with less than 25% of the craft brewery owned or controlled by an alcoholic beverage industry member who is not themselves a craft brewer. Finally, a craft brewer must be traditional. A traditional brewer has either an all

malt primary beer (the beer that represents the greatest volume among that brewer's brands) or has at least 50% of its volume in either all malt beers or in beers that use adjuncts to enhance rather than lighten flavor. Adjuncts, like rice or corn, add sugar to the brewing process, but no flavor or color and are traditionally less expensive. The Abita Brewing Company meets all three of the requirements to be considered a craft brewer.

The major brewing companies didn't take the microbrewing movement seriously at first. However, beer drinkers were beginning to shift their loyalties. Momentum began to change in the early 1990s when the annual volume growth of craft beer began increasing. It kept increasing every year, reaching a high in 1995. Microbreweries, brew pubs, different beer types and brands swept the country. By 1998 American craft beer was available just about everywhere. Currently, growth of the craft beer industry is 12% by volume and 16% in dollars, and more than 8 million barrels of craft beer were enjoyed by discriminating palates in the United States in 2007.

Abita Brewing Company is among the top 20 craft brewers in the nation and the largest and oldest craft brewer in the Southeast.

One of the first 6-packs of Abita Amber.
The top labels were hand applied.

HISTORY OF ABITA BEER

When two local entrepreneurs began home-brewing beer as a hobby, little did they dream that their avocation would eventually turn into a company that would grow from its first production of 1,500 barrels in 1986, to a multi-million dollar brewing operation that donates more beer each year to non-profit organizations than they brewed in year number one.

That's how it all got started for Abita Beer. The very first beer was brewed in Abita Springs, a small community nestled in the piney woods about 30 miles north of New Orleans, for a good reason – the water source. The crystal clear Abita Springs water is the most perfect water for beer. The small microbrewery began in a humble building that is now home to the Abita Brew Pub, a popular local restaurant and pub, but had to move up the road in 1994 to its current site to keep up with the demand for their product. The brewery has expanded numerous times since that first move.

"It's always been about the beer first," said David Blossman, President of Abita Beer. "That's why you see so many varieties. We like to make them, we like to try different things and make great beer. People tell us it's bad business, and it would be more profitable for us to just be an Amber beer factory, but we would get bored."

Abita's first beers were Amber and Golden. Abita Amber is by far the company's most popular brand, but the brewery makes at least two dozen different products throughout the year, including seven that are offered at all times. Abita's "Flagship" brews include Amber, Restoration Pale Ale, Golden, Jockamo I.P.A., Light, Purple Haze and Turbodog (first produced for an Abita birthday party in 1989). Many of Abita's other brews are produced in very small batches for its "Select" program, available only in kegs. Purple Haze, Abita's raspberry beer, was developed from age-old fruit-flavored ales that were enjoyed in Europe, especially Belgium, though Abita's version, a wheat beer, is a departure from those traditions. It was introduced in the mid-1990s when many other small breweries were testing the market's waters for fruit-flavored beers. Most of these passed by the wayside, but Purple Haze has continued as a highly successful product for Abita. Blossman credits that to using a seedless raspberry puree, rather than the artificial flavors or concentrates used by others. Abita Pecan Harvest and Abita Strawberry Harvest are made with real Louisiana nuts and berries.

Even Abita's non-alcoholic root beer bears the stamp of a craft brewer. The drink is made with herbs, vanilla and yucca (which creates the foam) and it is sweetened with Louisiana sugar cane rather than the corn syrups that are the standard of the large soft-drink makers. The root beer is hot mixed, and there's no caffeine in Abita Root Beer – it would have to be artificially added to the soft drink and that's not the Abita way.

"We're one of the only breweries in the world that doesn't need to treat their water. That means there are no chemicals, no interference with the water, and that's why it has the right pH balance and minerals," says Blossman. "I'd put it up against any water in the world."

The Abita Brewing Company is the oldest and largest craft brewer in the Southeast. Abita is the 30th largest commercial brewer by production volume in the nation and the 17th largest craft brewer in the United States.

ast the perfec-
est serve-with-
lanet.
that sits
ouisiana
waukee?

Fish
that's
ss the
s is
ita
the
ries
ders
ing
hem
wers

rings
gend.
amed
loosely
er." Since the
long before,

dark, and tinged by chocolate malt—it's
not a beginner's beer. Not surprising,

though, that it's developed a following
among a population known worldwide

the restauran
malt, hops a
have wor
quality

The S
The o
is the
the D
which I
reinventi
roughest b
has hung in t
any brewery i
still produces
many credit its
with bringi
21
ba
19
ers
up wi
the awa
Voodoo Lager
of experimen
secured a loca

The pavilion in the Abita Springs Tourist park. Originally built for the Orleans Cotton Centennial Exposition of 1884, it was later moved to Abita Springs. Funds raised by Abita Restoration Pale Ale helped restore the pavilion after Hurricane Katrina.

The 125 foot tower atop the Falstaff Brewery was a weather forecasting beacon for New Orleans residents.
Courtesy of the Historic New Orleans Collection.

HISTORY OF BEER
IN NEW ORLEANS

If not for the German community of old New Orleans, we wouldn't be reading this cookbook today. German immigrants introduced beer as an everyday drink to the city. Wine had been the primary beverage preferred by the French, and it was far pricier than beer.

Prior to 1850, a horrible beverage called "city beer" was consumed by the average working man in New Orleans. It was made of fermented molasses and vermouth and had no preservatives and spoiled quickly. Real beer was brewed in Pittsburgh, Milwaukee and St. Louis and imported into New Orleans. Problems occurred because of the lack of climate control. In the winter, the barrels of beer froze on the way to New Orleans. In the summer heat, the barrels would explode. Newspaper stories tell of crafty beer drinkers running out to the riverfront with mugs and pitchers to scoop up the brew from the "beer bust" on the wharf.

THE FIRST BEER BREWED IN NEW ORLEANS

In 1864, just before the Civil War, tavern owner George Merz successfully brewed the first lager beer in New Orleans. Cooling is necessary to brew a lager and Merz shipped ice all the way from Maine to accomplish this amazing feat in the history of brewing. The ice was hand-sawed from lakes and rivers in the state of Maine, packed in sawdust to insulate it and shipped to New Orleans. This process continued for 15 years until refrigeration and insulated ice houses came about in 1879, making it possible for lager beer breweries to really take hold in New Orleans.

The Merz Brewery on Toulouse Street in New Orleans from the 1867 city directory. *Courtesy of the Louisiana Collection, Earl K. Long Library, University of New Orleans.*

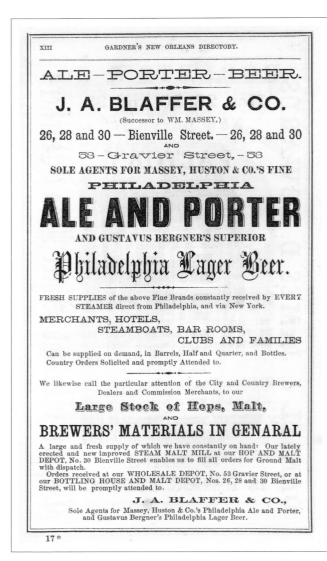

MODERN BREWERIES COME TO TOWN

About thirty breweries were listed in the city directory from 1850 to the turn of the century. New Orleans was once proclaimed "the brewing capital of the South" in the days before the 18th Amendment (also known as Prohibition) was passed into law in 1920. There was stiff competition for the beer drinker's dollar.

The first was the Southern Brewery, located in the French Quarter. Another favorite was the Standard Brewery, which began operation in the late 1800s. The newspaper described Standard's brewery as a place where "only the best material, hops, malt and other ingredients are used and the beer is of superior quality". The American Brewery Company made Regal Beer in 1891 on the site where the Royal Sonesta Hotel now stands. The Columbia Brewery was located at the corner of Elysian Fields and Chartres and their daily output was 180 barrels of beer per day.

THE BEER GARDENS OF NEW ORLEANS

Many of the larger breweries owned and operated beer gardens in and around the city. These gardens were more like parks than saloons and often whole families would gather for the evening. Folks brought along a picnic lunch and dined under the trees. In the evening, family dances were held in the pavilions. The Tivoli Gardens, one of the largest beer gardens, was located on Bayou St. John, which was on the outskirts of town in 1853. Beer was just ten cents a serving.

In 1853 The Tivoli Gardens was located at Basin Street and Bayou St. John and was one of the largest beer gardens in the area. *Courtesy of the Historic New Orleans Collection.*

Paul Cavailler del. et Litho.

Litho X. Magny, Passage de la Bourse

Workers in the Jackson Brewing Company in 1948.
Courtesy of the Historic New Orleans Collection.

24
JAX BREWERY
FEB-26-1948

Two Jax beer trucks parked near Jackson Square. The company was named for the square and its namesake, Andrew Jackson. *Courtesy of the Historic New Orleans Collection.*

Checking the wort at the Falstaff Brewery.
Courtesy of the Historic New Orleans Collection.

THE JAX BREWERY

The most successful beer baron of New Orleans was Lawrence Fabacher, who owned the Jax Brewery on Decatur Street, founded in 1890. The company was named for Jackson Square and its namesake, Andrew Jackson. Jax Beer was the most widely consumed beer in New Orleans, and the Jackson Brewery was the largest independent brewery in the South and the tenth largest single-plant brewery in the nation.

Fabacher was a wealthy and well-known character in New Orleans, with a mansion on St. Charles Avenue. His home had a marble saltwater swimming pool, a gym, stables, a greenhouse, fish ponds, sunken gardens and quarters for 13 live-in servants.

During Prohibition many breweries were forced to close, but the Jackson Brewery stayed in operation by manufacturing near beer and other beverages, such as root beer. The brewery closed in 1974. The brewery building still stands today, converted to a shopping area and tourist attraction.

FALSTAFF

The National Brewing Company was located at 2600 Gravier Street, near the parish prison. It was bought by Falstaff in 1936 and remained in operation until 1978. The Falstaff facility on Gravier Street may be remembered as a weather forecasting beacon. In 1952, a 125-foot tower was added to the top of the brewery. The tower was a vertical electrical sign spelling out "Falstaff" with a large ball on top. The ball would light up green if fair, red if cloudy, red and white if raining, and flashing red and white if storms were approaching. The letters spelling out "Falstaff" signaled the temperature; they flashed on and off if the temperature was constant and lit from top to bottom if temperatures were falling and from bottom to top if rising. The Falstaff building and tower remain and are currently being renovated into a condominium complex.

DIXIE

Valentine Merz opened The Dixie Brewing Company in 1907 on Halloween Day. Dixie was housed in a beautiful new brick building on Tulane Avenue that was equipped with $85,000 worth of modern brewing equipment. Dixie hung on through Prohibition and began brewing beer again in 1934. One of their more memorable beers was Dixie 45. The name was coined by Nick's Bar, across the street from the brewery. Nick said that Dixie had a kick like a "45" revolver. The brewery added the number until another brand, Colt 45, came out. In the 1970s, Dixie continued brewing while both Jax and Falstaff went out of business.

THE PROCESS
OF MAKING BEER

HOW WE MAKE ABITA BEER

THE INGREDIENTS

There are really only four main ingredients in Abita Beer: water, barley, hops and yeast. Just four simple ingredients combine to create more than a dozen very different brews. Nothing artificial ever goes into Abita Beer; we use only all natural ingredients. The precise recipe and timing of the brews are controlled by the Brewmaster and the result is the wonderful variety of Abita beers you've come to know and love.

WATER

Let's start with the water. It's the reason the Abita Brewing Company is located in beautiful Abita Springs, Louisiana. While most other breweries must filter and chemically treat their water for the brewing process, Abita needs neither; we take our water straight from the source. Our water is drawn from a deep artesian well in the Southern Hills aquifer system. More than 3,000 feet deep in some areas, it contains fresh water kept pristine in underground structures that are more than five million years old. Our water has been tested and shown to be free of man-made pollutants, including Tritium, a man-made radioactive isotope that marks all surface waters. Being free of Tritium means no surface waters — and the pollution they bring with them — have infiltrated our artesian well.

Since its days as a Choctaw Indian settlement, Abita's spring water has been a cherished natural resource. The Choctaws used it for medicinal purposes, and tourists at the turn of the 20th century flocked to the springs to "take the water" and recuperate from yellow fever.

HOW BEER GOT HERE

The first beer may have happened by accident...but what a wonderful accident it was for thirsty people everywhere. No one can say how the first yeast found its way into a sugar-water mixture and started doing what comes naturally — creating a bubbly concoction with an alcoholic kick to it. Here's the science of fermentation: yeast consumes sugar and makes alcohol and carbon dioxide. You get beer when yeast consumes the sugar from grains. You end up with wine when yeast consumes the sugar in fruit. Both beverages have been consumed for thousands of years to the delight of generations. Raise a glass to the magic of yeast and the clever cave brewers of prehistoric times.

The ancient Sumarians drank beer more than 6,000 years ago. They dubbed their brand of brew the "divine drink". The Babylonians brewed 20 different types of beer. They sipped their unfiltered beer through straws to avoid drinking the bitter brewing residue.

Until the Middle Ages, brewing beer was strictly women's work because it was closely associated with baking bread. Later, Monks living in monasteries took over the brewing of beer as a source of "liquid bread" that could be consumed during fasting periods. The excess beer was sold to the public in monastery pubs and the refined art of brewing was born.

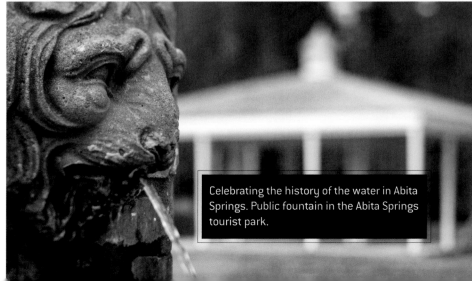

Celebrating the history of the water in Abita Springs. Public fountain in the Abita Springs tourist park.

A story is told of a young Spaniard named Henriques who lived in Louisiana during the late 1790s. While hunting along the shores of Lake Pontchartrain, he met a beautiful Choctaw girl and persuaded the chief to allow them to marry. After bringing her home to New Orleans, Henriques watched his wife grow pale and weak, and soon he realized that she was very ill.

None of the local doctors could cure her so Henriques finally consulted the Choctaws' medicine man. The young woman was carried to the spring and left there with only a hammock, food and a dipper to drink from the spring. When Henriques returned, to his amazement, his wife was totally well and the water's fame as a curative began to spread.

Word of the wonderful water spread to neighboring communities and in 1887, the first railroad arrived to the area. Boarding houses, hotels and restaurants were soon constructed to accommodate visitors. In 1903, the town of Abita Springs was formally organized, and chartered in 1912.

Take a sip from one of the water fountains inside the Abita Brewery and you are tasting the same pure water we pump from the ancient source for our beer. There's no place like home when it comes to brewing Abita Beer.

BARLEY

The stalks you see on the Abita logo are not wheat, but good old barley. Barley can be eaten as a grain and it is sometimes used in soups and stews. Barley is good for you — it's full of fiber. Barley is also very good for something else: making beer. Barley is to beer as grapes are to wine. But before the barley goes into Abita Beer, it must be malted.

Malting is a way of processing any cereal grain. Here's how it works: Grains of barley are seeds. The barley seed is moistened, and like any other seed, it begins to grow.

The barley is then quickly heated in a large oven, called a kiln, to stop the growing process.

Malting the barley develops the enzymes in the grain that are needed to turn barley starch into barley sugar. Malted barley is also used to make scotch whiskey and malt vinegar. Barley gets the malting treatment more than any other grain because it has a thick outer husk that stands up to all that soaking, sprouting and roasting. The wheat in our Abita Wheat seasonal brew is malted, too. Malting is a complicated process and takes years of training and experience to master.

Abita acquires their barley already malted. We use only two row barley grown specifically for brewing. Two row refers to the way barley kernels are arranged on the stalk. Two row barley has a fuller, maltier flavor than inferior six row varieties. Seems picky, but we want the best for our beer. We search the world for the very best and currently use barley from North America, the United Kingdom and Germany. Our malt varieties include Pale, Crystal, Lager, Wheat and Chocolate Malt as well as numerous specialty malts.

HOPS

Hops are the flowers of the hop plant and contain essential oils. They grow on a climbing vine and look more like a small, green pinecone than a rose or a daisy. Hops are often grown in areas that also produce wine grapes, such as the Willamette and Yuchana valleys in the Pacific Northwest. They balance the sweetness of the malted barley, they are a natural preservative and they add flavors and aromas to the brew. Alpha acids in the hops determine the bitterness content. Hops can be described with words like "grassy," "floral," "citrus," "spicy," "piney" and "earthy." Hop flavor is subtle in most beers.

Hops are used at three different stages in the beer making process. Bittering hops are added first to offset natural sweetness. During the boiling process, flavoring hops are added to give a well-rounded hop flavor and aroma. At the

Hops, along with three of the many varieties of malt used in making Abita Beer: Pale, Crystal and Chocolate.

end of the boil, even more hops are added for additional aromas in the finished beer. To get a stronger taste of the hops, try an Abita Restoration Pale Ale or an Abita Jockamo I.P.A.

YEAST
Yeast is a single-celled microorganism that converts sugar into two by-products: alcohol and carbon dioxide. We call that neat trick fermentation. Yeast has been used for making bread and beer for thousands of years.

There are two types of yeast: ale and lager. Lagers ferment from the bottom of the tank at colder temperatures and make a smoother, more well-rounded beer. Ales ferment from the top at warmer temperatures and make a beer with more esters. Esters are compounds that produce pleasant aromas like fruit and cloves. Abita uses several kinds of specialized brewers' yeasts from around the world, including German Lager, German Ale, Belgian Ale, Californian Ale and other specialty yeasts that are cultivated in labs specifically for Abita Beer.

AND SOMETHING EXTRA
The entire brewing process is computer monitored and automated to ensure the quality and consistency of Abita Beer. That being said...we couldn't make Abita Beer without the great people who work at the brewery.

Our employees are beer people. They truly love brewing and are passionately involved in the process in a hands-on way that no computer can match. New brews are always being created and tested. Approximately 50 people are involved in the process of brewing your Abita Beer and making sure it gets to you.

THE PROCESS

THE MASH
Here's where we get down to business. The malted barley is ground to expose the starches and now we call it grist. The grist is mixed with warm water in a stainless-steel vessel called the Mash Tun and the mixture is called the Mash.

As the temperature rises in the Mash Tun, the enzymes in the grist break down the starches into sugars. The difference in mash temperature makes either simple sugars that are fully fermented into alcohol and carbon dioxide (CO_2) by yeast or complex sugars that are not fully fermented and give body and sweetness to the beer. This process takes about two hours and results in a sweet concoction that is then transferred to a different "tun" with a special name.

THE WORT
The Mash is now transferred to the Lauter Tun. The main feature of the Lauter Tun is the perforated false bottom on the tank — sort of like a strainer or colander. The sweet liquid is called the First Wort and it is drained from the mash and collected.

After the First Wort is drained away, the bed of grain at the top of the Lauter Tun is sprayed with hot water. This process is called the Sparge. Sparging rinses and extracts the remaining sugars and flavors from the mash. Sparging is a very delicate process. The pH of the wort and the temperature of the sparge water must be carefully controlled or excess tannins will be released into the wort. Tannins are natural chemical compounds found in beer. Too much tannin can give the beer an overly dry and bitter taste and affect the clarity of the brew. The First and Second Wort are combined and transferred into a brew kettle for boiling.

THE BOIL
When you boil water on the stove at home, heat is applied to the bottom of the pot and the entire contents of the pot must be gradually heated until it reaches boiling temperature. The more liquid in the pot, the longer it takes to boil.

The Abita Brewing Company was the first brewery outside Europe to use a revolutionary new boiling system called the Merlin. It reduces the boiling time from 90 minutes to 35 minutes and is 70% more energy efficient. It works by moving the wort over a heated cone inside the Merlin, quickly bringing it up to the proper temperature. Have you ever seen one of those cold-drink dispensers where the lemonade or fruit punch is circulated like a fountain over a cone inside a clear glass container? The chilled cone in the drink dispenser is cooling the drink and also making a pretty display. Inside the Merlin, the heated cone is boosting the temperature of the wort and speeding up the beer-brewing process.

Hops are introduced into the wort at three different stages in the boiling process. Bittering hops are added first to offset the natural sweetness of the wort. During the boiling process, flavoring hops are added to give a well-rounded hop flavor and aroma. At the end of the boil, even more hops are added for additional aromas in the finished beer.

The brewmaster can test the aroma potential of different hops by brewing up some "hop tea". The hops are steeped in hot water and the different aromas are evaluated. The brewmaster uses a very sensitive instrument for this process called "his nose". No mechanical device can replace a first-class human nose.

Once the boiling process is completed, the wort is run through a whirlpool to separate the solids from the liquids. Proteins and hops are spun out and clear wort remains.

The wort is still very hot and needs to be cooled before the yeast is added. In the heat exchanger hot wort passes over pipes filled with cold water. The water is heated and the wort is cooled to anywhere from 50 to 70 degrees depending on the type of beer being made. The final temperature of the wort must be just right or the yeast can't begin the process of fermentation.

FERMENTATION

Yeast is now added to the wort and the liquid is moved to a large stainless-steel fermentation vessel. At this stage we call the product...beer.

The yeast goes right to work eating the malt sugar and creating alcohol and CO_2. If you were to look down into the fermentation tank, you would actually see the beer bubbling. The process takes anywhere from four to 14 days, depending upon the beer being brewed. During this time, the CO_2 is allowed to escape from the tank but the alcohol remains. When 85% of the sugars have been eaten up by the hungry yeast, the fermentation vessel is closed to capture the remaining CO_2 to give the beer natural carbonation.

The type of yeast used during fermentation determines whether a beer is an ale or a lager. We select different strains of yeast from the thousands available for each recipe we develop. The next step in the brewing process is aging.

When fermentation is complete, the yeast is then drained from the tank and is used again to brew more beer. Some beers are transferred into a secondary aging tank where more hops are added — this process is called dry hopping and it gives the brew a more pronounced hop flavor and aroma. Jockamo I.P.A., Restoration Pale Ale, Red Ale and our Christmas Ale are among the ones that are dry hopped.

AGING

The beer ages in the cold, dark stainless-steel tanks for a minimum of 14 days up to three months. The temperature inside the climate-controlled tanks drops to 32 degrees. Amber, Golden, Restoration Pale Ale and Jockamo are aged for a minimum of 14 days. Abita Light is aged for a minimum of 21 days and Andygator ages for 45 days. During the aging process, the yeast settles and separates from the beer.

FILTERING

At the end of the aging period, the beer is filtered. Abita uses a two-part filtration process. First, we centrifuge filter the beer, spinning out 95% of the remaining yeast and microproteins. We filter the beer again through a Plate and Frame sheet filter to finish the job and clarify the beer, making it bright. Now, the moment we've been waiting for — the beer is ready to drink, so let's get it to packaging.

BOTTLING

The beer is transferred to a "Bright" beer tank and is bottled or kegged. Our bottling line is capable of producing 160 bottles per minute. They are rinsed, purged of air, pressure filled, capped, labeled and grouped into six-packs. Every bottle is laser dated for freshness. The bottles and kegs are cold stored for no more than seven days before they are shipped in our climate-controlled trucks to our distributors. Who's ready for a beer? Cheers.

HOW TO ENJOY BEER

YOU PROBABLY DON'T NEED ANYONE TO TELL YOU HOW TO ENJOY BEER.
BUT JUST IN CASE…HERE ARE A FEW TIPS, TRICKS AND SUGGESTIONS.

WHAT ABITA BREWS & HOW YOU PAIR IT WITH FOOD

Although wine comes to mind when trying to pair your favorite food with strong drink, don't rule out pairing beer with a great selection of foods. Like wine, beer has different flavors, aromas, subtleties and aftertastes. In fact, beer stands up very well to many strongly flavored foods that wine just can't handle. Unlike wine and liquor, the carbonation in beer lifts the oils and fats from the tongue and refreshes the palate.

Don't get hung up on rules when choosing what style of beer pairs with which foods. Wine experts can be a little snobby and their rules are strict. But, beer lovers just want everyone to be happy and enjoy their meal. Plus, every person's palate is a little bit different, so let your taste buds be your guide. Abita makes dozens of brews and there's sure to be one (or more if it is a multi-course meal) that is a perfect partner to your meal. You can even blend different Abita beers to create new tastes. Visit our website, (Abita.com), for beer mixing recipes and instructions. We've made pairing recommendations for each recipe and if the seasonal choice is not available, you can always substitute Amber for Fall Fest, Golden or Light for Wheat and Turbodog for Christmas Ale.

WARM BEER IS NOT A CRIME

Beer drinkers in other countries sometimes scoff at the American tradition of serving cold beer. However, it is true that the temperature of a beer does have an influence on your drinking experience. Colder temperatures allow beers like pale lagers to be enjoyed for their crispness; while warmer temperatures let you experience the more rounded flavors of an ale. We've provided our serving temperature suggestions for each Abita brew later on in this section.

THE THREE C'S OF BEER

It may take a little time and some experimenting to learn about the nuances of the Abita beers, but it will be time well spent. When purchasing a diamond, experts follow the "four C's"– cut, color, carats and clarity. In beer and food pairing, you can follow one of the "three C's" – cut, complement or contrast.

CUT

Choose a beer that cuts through a powerful food flavor and refreshes your palate. Beers can cut the spicy flavor of Mexican or Thai food. Try a beer that cuts the richness of fatty fried foods or cuts through the sweetness of a dessert.

COMPLEMENT

Select a beer that has some of the same attributes as the food you are serving – fruit flavors with fruit, spicy beers with spicy food, big robust brews with red meats and flavorful cheeses. If you used a beer in the recipe, you can also serve it with the meal.

CONTRAST

Do a U-turn and choose a beer that counter-balances your food choice. For example, a strong and flavorful brew paired with a delicate salad or sushi.

(Left to Right)
Andygator, Turbodog, Jockamo I.P.A., Amber,
Golden, Root Beer, Abbey Ale & Purple Haze

MOVING BEYOND THE BEER KOOZIE

A bottle of Abita Beer wrapped in a foam beer koozie is a fine thing. The beer stays nice and cold and doesn't sweat on the furniture. Abita Beer is already packaged in an environmentally friendly bottle that uses less glass than traditional long-necks. The glass is brown to protect the contents from sunlight, which can damage the flavor of the beer. However, there are a variety of beer glasses that can enhance the enjoyment of your Abita beverage. In fact, glassware is important to tasting each style. The right glass can enhance the aroma, show off the appearance or keep your hand from warming the beer.

The pouring process has an influence on a beer's presentation, too. The rate of flow from the tap or bottle, the angle of the glass and position of the pour (into the center or down the side of the glass) makes a difference. Start with a "beer clean" glass. When beer glasses are washed with other dishes an invisible layer of film is deposited. These residues attack the foam and give the beer an "off" taste. You can tell a glass is not beer clean when CO_2 bubbles cling to the bottom and sides of a glass. Hand wash beer glasses apart from other dishes with a non-foaming detergent. Rinse thoroughly and air dry upside down on a wire rack. Then prepare your glass for drinking by rinsing it with 1/2 ounce of beer. Agitate the beer and swirl the foam inside the glass before discarding. The bubbles clean the surface and remove any soap or other beverage residue.

WHEAT BEER GLASS
Also known as Weizenbier or Weißbier. Taller than a pint glass, it is narrow at the bottom and slightly wider at the top. Sometimes confused with a pilsner glass, the wheat glass has a bigger curve from top to bottom. Choose this glass to showcase the beer's color and allow room for the beer's head.

PINT GLASS
The American pint glass found in most American establishments is cone shaped and wider at the top than the base. This glass is popular because it holds a lot of beer, is easy to hold in your hand and can be stored in stacks. The English or Imperial pint glass is bigger, holds more liquid than the American pint and has a rounded shape near the rim.

BEER STEIN
A beer stein is a tankard or mug and can be made of pewter, silver, wood, porcelain, earthenware or glass. It can have a hinged lid that is lifted with your thumb. The lid was popular on steins during the time of the Black Plague, to prevent diseased flies from getting into your beer. Yuck!

PILSNER GLASS

Many different beers have been poured into a pilsner glass but it was intended for its namesake, the pilsner. Pilsner glasses are generally smaller than pint glasses and showcase the color, effervescence and clarity of the beer.

FLUTE GLASS

Like a champagne flute, this style of glass helps maintain carbonation and concentrates the aroma.

GOBLET OR CHALICE

These are stemmed, bowl-shaped glasses. Goblets are more delicate while the Chalice is made of heavy thick glass. Some chalices are even etched on the bottom to attract carbon dioxide and provide a stream of bubbles to maintain a nice head on the beer.

SNIFTERS

Usually chosen for serving brandy and cognac, a snifter is sometimes chosen for aromatic beers. The shape allows you to swirl the beer and produce intense aromas.

TULIP GLASS

A tulip glass resembles a tumbler that flares out to form a lip. Plenty of room for a head and to savor the aroma.

STANGE

It means "stick" or "bar" in German and that's what it looks like. It's a traditional German beer glass.

ENJOYING BEER

THE TASTING TEST

There are five distinct taste qualities that the taste buds on your tongue can detect. They are sweet, salty, sour, bitter and umami. Whoa...what's that last one? Umami (pronounced YOU-mommy) is the Japanese word for a savory taste found in tomatoes, Parmesan cheese, mushrooms and many Asian foods. It is a recent edition to the group of taste qualities and the subject of some controversy among scientists and flavor specialists who study this kind of stuff.

You may remember testing various areas of your tongue in grade school to determine the "tongue map". We are supposed to be able to perceive sweet tastes at the tip of our tongue, bitter at the back and other tastes in different places. If you were never able to get the right tastes in proper places at the science fair, don't feel bad. New research shows that we perceive all the taste qualities all over our tongue, although some areas may be more sensitive to certain qualities than others. Try recreating that science fair moment for yourself with your favorite Abita.

When tasting a beer for the first time, don't swallow immediately. Let the beer rest in your mouth and contact all those taste buds. Try to detect some of those five flavor qualities. As you swallow the beer, breathe out through your nose to taste more flavors. Much of what we taste is determined by our sense of smell. Odor molecules travel into your nose and transmit information to the olfactory bulb in your brain. Of course, beer is a multi-sensory experience, so read on to learn more about the smells, sights and sounds of enjoying Abita Beer.

THE BEER FLAVOR WHEEL

When people who enjoy beer talk about their favorites, you'll hear some of the same words over and over. Terms like mouthfeel, aromatic, grassy or hoppy have become part of the standard language of beer. In the 1970s, Dr. Morten Meilgaard created the Beer Flavor Wheel. The wheel has 14 categories broken down into 44 flavors. The wheel was a way to standardize a language through which beer tasters can agree on a word-to-flavor correlation.

Scientists have found more than 1,000 identifiable flavors in beer, yet an experienced taster can pick out perhaps only 100.

Dr. Morten's wheel gave beer tasters a common vocabulary that caught on all over the world. It is now used as the standard reference by the European Brewery Convention, the American Society of Brewing Chemists, and the Master Brewers Association of the Americas.

BEER FLAVOR WHEEL

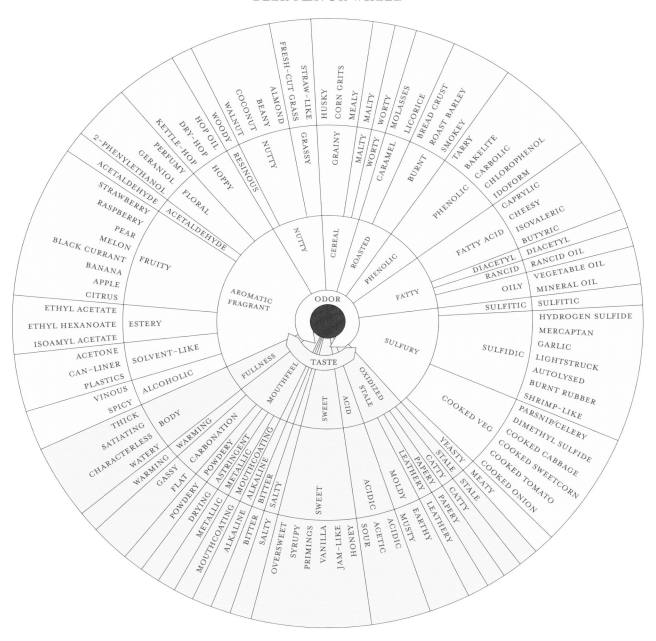

BEER COLOR

The way a beer looks has a powerful impact on its enjoyment. The color of a beer is an important visual cue and part of the overall sensory appeal of evaluating a brew. Brewers carefully control the color of their beers and define the colors on the Lovibond scale. The higher the number, the darker the color of the beer. Abita Wheat is a 3 and Turbodog is a 60 on the Lovibond scale.

Classic beer styles are defined in part by definite visual images of what is appropriate.

Larger breweries use a special device called a spectrophotometer to measure the exact Lovibond units. If you don't have your own personal spectrophotometer, you can simply compare the tall, cold glass of beer you're holding to the chart below.

BEER HUES IN LOVIBOND UNITS

	BASIC COLOR	HUE	LOVIBOND UNITS
3	YELLOW	LIGHT	2.0 - 3.0
		MEDIUM	3.0 - 4.5
		DEEPSTRAW/GOLD	4.5 - 6.0
6		DEEP GOLD	6.0 - 7.5
	AMBER	LIGHT	7.5 - 9.0
		COPPER	9.0 - 11
12		RED/BROWN	11 - 14
	BROWN	LIGHT	14 - 17
		MEDIUM	17 - 20
		DARK-LIGHT BLACK	20 - 25
20	BLACK	START OF FULL BLACK	>25

BEER BITTERNESS

Beer is also rated in units of bitterness called International Bitterness Units or IBUs. IBUs measure the intensity of the bitterness of the beer. Bitterness in beer comes from a compound in hops called alpha acids. Different varieties of hops have different ranges of alpha. Brewers use different varieties and quantities of hops to create different levels of bitterness.

The chart below is often used in beer tasting competitions and displays the range in color and the range in bitterness for many different beer varieties.

COLOR & BITTERNESS COMPARISON CHART

LOVIBOND UNITS		BITTERNESS IBU	COLOR LOVIBOND UNITS	LOVIBOND UNITS		BITTERNESS IBU	COLOR LOVIBOND UNITS
1	LIGHT LAGER	5-15	1.5-4	7	VIENNA-STYLE LAGER	22-28	8-12
	WHEAT ALE	10-35	2-10		ESB (EXTRA SPECIAL BITTER)	30-55	8-14
	BELGIAN WHITE	10-17	2-4		SCOTTISH ALE	9-20	8-17
	LAGER	5-14	2-4		ENGLISH MILD ALE	10-24	8-17
2	ICE LAGER	10-22	2-5	12	ENGLISH/SCOTTISH STRONG ALE	30-65	8-21
	MALT LIQUOR	12-23	2-5		DARK LAGER	22-30	8-30
	WEIZEN BEER	3-15	2-9		DUNKELWEIZEN	10-15	10-19
	OKTOBERFEST/MARZEN	7-25	2-15		SCOTCH ALE	25-35	10-25
3	PILSNER	20-40	3-6	17	AMBER/RED ALE	30-40	11-18
	BLONDE/GOLDEN ALE	15-25	3-7		IRISH ALE	20-28	11-18
	BELGIAN-STYLE TRIPLE ALE	20-25	3.5-7		DUSSELDORF-STYLE ALTBEIR	25-48	11-19
4	BELGIAN-STYLE ALE-PALE STRONG	20-50	3.5-7	22	BARLEYWINE	40-100	11-22
	HEFEWEIZEN	10-35	3-10		CALIFORNIA COMMON BEER	35-45	12-17
	KÖLSH	18-25	4-7		OLD ALE	30-65	12-30
	HELLES BOCK/MAIBOCK PALE LAGER	20-38	4-10		BELGIAN-STYLE DUBBEL ALE	18-25	14-18
5	CREAM ALE	18-25	4-15	27	MUNICH DUNKEL	18-28	14-28
	ENGLISH PALE ALE	20-40	5-14		BROWN ALE	15-45	15-22
	FRUIT OR VEGETABLE BEER	5-70	5-50		BOCK	20-30	20-30
	HERB & SPICE BEER	5-70	5-50		PORTER	20-40	20-35
6	AMERICAN PALE ALE	28-40	6-14	32	OATMEAL STOUT	20-40	20+
	INDIA PALE ALE (AM OR ENG)	35-65	6-14		IMPERIAL STOUT	50-80	20+
	AMBER LAGER	18-30	6-14		STOUT	30-60	40+
7	LAMBIC	11-23	6-25	37	IRISH DRY STOUT	30-40	40+
	DOPPELBOCK	16-30	6-25		MILK STOUT	15-25	40+

ABITA FLAGSHIP BREWS

The Abita Brewing Company produces these seven beers all year long. These rich, wonderfully flavored brews are enjoyed year round in restaurants, bars, festivals and get-togethers throughout Louisiana and across the country.

AMBER

Amber is a Munich-style lager brewed with crystal malt and Perle hops. It has a smooth, malty, slightly caramel flavor and a rich amber color. Abita Amber was the first beer offered by the brewery and continues to be our leading seller. Amber is Abita's most versatile beer for pairing with food. It has been voted "best beer" in numerous New Orleans reader polls and is used frequently in recipes of great Louisiana chefs.

Because of its smooth, malty flavor, try it with smoked sausages, Louisiana boudin, or even with caviar. It's great with crawfish, grilled seafood and Cajun food. You also might enjoy it paired with a spicy gumbo or tomato-based pasta sauce. It also goes well with fried catfish dipped in a tart, lemony tartar sauce. Parmesan, Pecorino and Romano cheeses are good parings with Abita Amber.

ABV 4.5%	IBU 17	Color 15	Calories 128	Carbs 10	Suggested Temp 40°

Suggested glasses: pint, pilsner or stein

LIGHT

Light is uniquely handcrafted using 100% all natural ingredients: malted barley, the finest hops, German lager yeast and pristine Abita Springs water. The result is the smoothest, most flavorful light beer you will ever taste. Great with almost anything, it's an excellent choice for lighter foods and salads, too. Try Abita Light with a sharp Cheddar cheese.

ABV 4.0%	IBU 10	Color 3	Calories 118	Carbs 8	Suggested Temp 38°

Suggested glasses: pint, pilsner or wheat

RESTORATION PALE ALE

Restoration Pale Ale was created after back-to-back hurricanes devastated Louisiana. With your help, the sales of the product raised over $550,000 for hurricane relief.

Restoration Pale Ale is made with Pale, Lager, Crystal and Cara Pils malted barley. It is liberally hopped and dry hopped with American Cascade and fermented with California Ale yeast. The end result is a brilliant gold ale with a rich body, mild bitterness and a snappy fresh citrus hop flavor and aroma. This beer can be paired with many different dishes according to your taste. The citrus flavor and aroma make it an excellent choice with most fish, especially ones that are prepared to match the flavor of the beer. American, Muenster, Havarti and Monterey Jack cheeses pair well with Restoration.

ABV 5.0%	IBU 20	Color 9	Calories 167	Carbs 15	Suggested Temp 42°

Suggested glasses: pint, pilsner, tulip or stein

JOCKAMO I.P.A.

Jockamo is named for the tribes of dancing, singing, chanting "Mardi Gras Indians" who have marched in New Orleans for over 250 years. When you hear the drums, join in the song…"Iko! Iko! Jockamo fe na ne".

Jockamo I.P.A. is a traditional India Pale Ale made with the best pale and light crystal malts that give the beer a copper color and malty flavor. This full-flavored beer is hopped and dry hopped liberally with Willamette and Columbus hops from the Pacific Northwest and has a 6.5% A.B.V. The spicy aroma of the hops contrasts nicely with the pleasant sweetness of the malts. Jockamo has a strong flavor that entices and excites the palate. The intense hop character adds more spice to a meal and makes it a good choice to team up with many spicy dishes. Cheddar and strong farmer cheeses stand up well to Jockamo's hoppy character. Jockamo goes well with wild game, grilled meats and Thai or Mexican cuisine.

ABV 6.5%	IBU 52	Color 16	Calories 190	Carbs 13	Suggested Temp 44°

Suggested glasses: pint, tulip or stein

ABITA FLAGSHIP BREWS

TURBODOG

Turbodog is a dark-brown ale brewed with Willamette hops and a combination of pale, crystal and chocolate malts. This combination gives Turbodog its rich body and color and a sweet chocolate toffee-like flavor. Turbodog began as a specialty ale but has gained a huge loyal following and has become one of our flagship brews.

This ale pairs well with most meats and is great served with hamburgers or sausages. It is a good match with smoked fish and can even stand up to wild game dishes. Turbodog also is great for marinating and braising meats and cooking such things as cabbage and greens. Colby, Gloucester, Cheddar and Blue cheeses go nicely with Turbodog. It's perfect with spicy Louisiana jambalaya or Spanish paella. Some even like it paired with chocolate!

ABV 5.6%	IBU 28	Color 60	Calories 168	Carbs 15	Suggested Temp 44°

Suggested glasses: pint, goblet, stange or stein

PURPLE HAZE

Purple Haze is a crisp, American-style wheat beer with raspberry puree added after filtration. Therefore, you may see raspberry pulp in the beer. The raspberries provide the lager with a subtle purple coloration and haze, a fruity aroma, and a tartly sweet taste.

This beer is best served with salads or paired with light fruit desserts, such as soufflés or chiffon cake. Many people enjoy it with chocolate desserts. Mascarpone cheese is used in many desserts and pairs well with Purple Haze or try some ripened Brie. It's also great with entrees prepared with fruit, especially citrus. Consider enjoying a Purple Haze alone at the end of your meal as dessert.

ABV 4.2%	IBU 13	Color 8	Calories 128	Carbs 11	Suggested Temp 38°

Suggested glasses: pint, pilsner, flute or tulip

GOLDEN

Golden is a crisp, clean continental lager. Just four ingredients are all it takes: American malt, Mt. Hood hops, German lager yeast and pure Abita Springs water. As the name applies, Abita Golden has a brilliant gold color. Its flavor makes this light lager the perfect match for Louisiana Creole food.

Both Abita Light and Abita Golden go well with just about anything. Try it with mild rice or pasta dishes, grilled vegetables, grilled chicken and fish, and even with something spicy like Louisiana boiled crawfish, shrimp and crabs. Goat cheeses like feta and chevre pair well with Abita Golden.

ABV 4.2%	IBU 11	Color 3	Calories 125	Carbs 10	Suggested Temp 38°

Suggested glasses: pint, pilsner or wheat

SEASONAL BREWS

Abita seasonal brews are available for a limited time. Each brew is custom created to perfectly match the time of year when they are enjoyed. As the calendar changes, Abita customers look forward to the return of each of their seasonal favorites.

BOCK

Bock (January – March) is the first of our seasonal brews. It is brewed with Perle hops and pale and caramel malts. Our Bock is similar to a German Maibock in its high malt content, full body and slightly higher alcohol content. Abita Bock is a very popular brew, especially during our Mardi Gras season. Gruyère, Emmental and Swiss are nice cheese choices with Bock. Great with roasted beef or pork. Try it with Mexican food, too.

ABV 6.5%	IBU 25	Color 13	Calories 187	Carbs 16	Suggested Temp 42°

Suggested glasses: pint, stein, goblet or stange

RED ALE

Red Ale (March – May) is brewed with pale and crystal malts, Sterling hops and an ale yeast from California. This ale has a rich ruby color, lacy collar, and pronounced caramel flavor. Try it with traditional Irish fare or a sweet and pleasant cow's milk cheese called Dubliner that can be found in most grocery stores.

ABV 5.2%	IBU 30	Color 16	Calories 151	Carbs 11	Suggested Temp 44°

Suggested glasses: pint, pilsner, tulip or stein

WHEAT

Wheat (May – September). German brewers discovered centuries ago that the addition of wheat produces a distinctively light, refreshing beer. Unlike traditional German wheat beers produced by other breweries, Abita Wheat is a lager, not an ale, and contains a generous amount of wheat which produces a clean, simple flavor. For a change of pace, try Abita Wheat with a twist of lemon. Feta and goat cheeses pair well with Wheat beer. Great with summertime fare such as pasta and salads, but don't forget barbecue and anything right off the grill.

ABV 4.2%	IBU 15	Color 3	Calories 125	Carbs 10	Suggested Temp 38°

Suggested glasses: wheat, pint or pilsner

FALL FEST

Fall Fest (September – November) is a Marzen-style Octoberfest lager. It is brewed with German Haullertau hops and pale and crystal malts. The result is a full-bodied, malty beer with a beautiful amber color. Celebrate the season with Abita Fall Fest and your favorite German food. Cheese pairings include Gruyère and Swiss-style cheeses.

ABV 5.4%	IBU 20	Color 12	Calories 167	Carbs 15	Suggested Temp 42°

Suggested glasses: pint, pilsner, goblet, stein or stange

CHRISTMAS ALE

Christmas Ale (November – December) rounds out our calendar. Generally, this beer is a dark ale, however, the recipe changes each year, offering a unique product crafted with special care. Enjoy your holidays with Abita Christmas Ale. The spicy character is excellent with traditional holiday foods such as gingerbread or spiced nuts. Try some Blue cheese or a creamy Camembert with a Christmas Ale.

Suggested Temp 44°

Suggested glasses: pint, tulip, snifter or stein

THE HARVEST BREWS

Every Abita Beer is made with the finest natural ingredients. The Harvest Brews are made with ingredients grown in Louisiana and picked at the height of the season to capture the most flavor for these unique brews. The Harvest Brews are available for a limited time and in limited quantities.

STRAWBERRY HARVEST LAGER

Strawberry Harvest Lager is a wheat beer made with real Louisiana strawberries, only picked late in the season when they're at their sweetest. This brew has earned quite a reputation in a short time, causing the brewery to up their production year after year. When this brew is found, e-mails and phone calls fly to friends informing them of the store's location. Strawberry Harvest is a crisp, light lager with just a hint of strawberry sweetness. Wonderful with desserts or lighter fare such as salads and pastas. Fresh cheeses such as Burrata, chevre, Creszenza, mozzarella or Teleme pair well with Strawberry Harvest.

ABV 4.2%	IBU 13	Color 5	Calories 128	Carbs 11	Suggested Temp 38°

Suggested glasses: pint, flute, snifter or tulip

PECAN HARVEST ALE

Pecan Harvest Ale is made with real Louisiana pecans that have been toasted to perfection. That is actually unique, as most beers with a nutty flavor or aroma aren't made with real nuts. The natural oils from the Louisiana pecans give the ale a light pecan finish and aroma. This ale is excellent served with both red meat and seafood, and no surprise here, it's also great with nuts! Try Pecan Harvest with Gouda cheese.

ABV 5.0%	IBU 20	Color 19	Calories 150	Carbs 11	Suggested Temp 44°

Suggested glasses: pint, flute, snifter or tulip

SPECIALTY BREWS

ANDYGATOR

Andygator, a creature of the swamp, is a unique high-gravity brew made with pale malt, German lager yeast and German Perle hops. Unlike other high-gravity brews, Andygator is fermented to a dry finish with a slightly sweet flavor and subtle fruit aroma. Reaching an alcohol strength of 8% by volume, it is a Helles Dopplebock.

You might find it goes well with fried foods. It pairs well with just about anything made with crawfish. Some like it with a robust sandwich. Gorgonzola and creamy Blue cheese are a good match with Andygator. Try serving it as an aperitif. Because of the high alcohol content, be cautious – sip it for the most enjoyment.

ABV 8.0%	IBU 25	Color 8	Calories 235	Carbs 19	Suggested Temp 42°

Suggested glasses: pint, goblet, stein, flute or snifter

ABBEY ALE

Abbey Ale honors the ancient tradition of monks who perfected the art of brewing beer to support the monastery and the brothers with their "liquid bread". We offer up our support and thank them with a 25¢ donation to St. Joseph's Abbey with every bottle of this heavenly brew. Dark amber in color, the aroma of caramel, fruits and cloves invite you to contemplate the creamy head of this "Dubbel" or double ale with an 8% ABV. Abita Abbey Ale is a malty brew, top-fermented and bottle aged to rapturous perfection.

Abbey Ale pairs well with meats, wild game, smoked foods, cheeses and even sushi. It is also an excellent dessert beer.

ABV 8.0%	IBU 32	Color 25	Calories 230	Carbs 18	Suggested Temp 46°

Suggested glasses: chalice, snifter, tulip

ABITA ROOT BEER

Abita Root Beer is made with a hot mix process using spring water, herbs, vanilla and yucca (which creates foam). Unlike most soft drink manufacturers, Abita sweetens its root beer with pure Louisiana cane sugar. The resulting taste is reminiscent of soft drinks made in the 1940s and 1950s, before bottlers turned to corn sugar and fructose. Some soft drink makers add caffeine to their product, but Abita is naturally caffeine-free.

Add a scoop of vanilla ice cream for an old-fashioned root beer float. Abita Root Beer can also be used in cooking to create delicious glazes and sauces as well as cakes and other desserts, or you can keep it simple – just pour it into a frosty mug and slurp loudly through a straw.

Suggested glasses: frosted stein

ABITA SELECT

Abita Select is an exclusive premium draft product line featuring a new style every few months. These specialty brews can be found only on tap, and only at certain restaurants and bars in Louisiana. Each Abita Select begins as a blank canvas for the brewers and allows them to experiment with new and different styles of beer. The wide variety of styles created displays the creativity and love of brewing that is at the heart of every Abita Beer.

PAST ABITA SELECT BREWS

Wit	Alt	Imperial Pilsner	Bohemian Pilsner
Four Grain	Cream Ale	Nut Brown Ale	Kristall Weizen
Saison	Hefe Weizen	Pale Ale	English Bitter
Rye	Doppelbock	Kolsch	Stout
Belgian Golden Ale	India Pale Ale (IPA)	Mocha Porter	

ABITA DINNER SERIES

The Abita Dinner Series was originated to celebrate the release of the newest Abita Select premium brew. These "Select" dinners were held every few months and paired Abita Select and other Abita brews with a gourmet meal. The dinners were so popular and well attended that the program has evolved and expanded so that more people can experience these fine dining events without waiting for the release of a Select brew. Dinner Series events have been held in New Orleans, Baton Rouge, Lafayette and even Chicago, New York and Atlanta. As the popularity of Abita Beer grows, so does the Abita Dinner Series.

Each course of the meal is paired with an Abita brew specially selected to enhance the dish. The complex flavors and aromas of each selected Abita Beer mingled with the unique food pairings is guaranteed to create an unforgettable gourmet experience. Discover an Abita Dinner Series near you at abita.com.

EXAMPLES OF PREVIOUS ABITA DINNER SERIES MENUS

Mr. B's Bistro	Galatoire's Bistro	Dickie Brennan's Steakhouse	NOLA Restaurant
WELCOME RECEPTION Fried Oysters Duck Springrolls Pairing – Amber	**WELCOME RECEPTION** Hand Passed Hors d'Oeuvres Pairing – Purple Haze	**WELCOME RECEPTION** Shrimp Beignets served with Chipotle Dipping Sauce Gulf Seafood Tartlets topped with Tarragon Crème Fraîche and Cajun Caviar Pairing – Amber	**WELCOME RECEPTION** Farmhouse Cheddar with Apple Smoked Bacon, Baby Greens, Louisiana Strawberries, Toasted Pistachios and Honey-Apple Vinaigrette Pairing – Wheat
I COURSE Gumbo Ya Ya A rich country-style gumbo made with chicken and andouille sausage. Pairing – Turbodog	**I COURSE** Oyster Soup Provençal Pairing – Abita Select Saison	**I COURSE** Exotic Gumbo served in French bread Pairing – Restoration Ale	**I COURSE** Tasso and Garlic Broiled Oysters on the Half Shell Pairing – Restoration Ale
II COURSE Demi Barbecued Shrimp Gulf shrimp barbecued New Orleans style, served in their shells with peppery butter sauce and French bread for dipping. Pairing – Restoration Ale	**II COURSE** Abita Amber BBQ Shrimp with Roasted Garlic Grits Pairing – Amber	**II COURSE** Soft Shell Crab served with Jumbo Lump Crabmeat, Peppery Arugula and Creole Mustard Bacon Vinaigrette Pairing – Purple Haze	**II COURSE** "Fish and Chips" Abita Battered Cod with Sweet Potato Fries, Vinegar and Spicy Aioli Pairing – Amber
III COURSE Veal Chop A 12-ounce wood grilled veal chop touched with smoked tomato butter sauce. Pairing – Abita Select Alt	**III COURSE** Crispy Skin on Snapper with a Roasted Pecan Meuniere Sauce Pairing – Pecan Harvest	**III COURSE** BBQ Rib-Eye served with Abita BBQ Shrimp and Yukon Gold Potato Purée Pairing – Abita Select Four Grain	**III COURSE** Purple Haze Glazed St. Louis Ribs with Baked Beans and Brie "Mac and Cheese" Pairing – Purple Haze
IV COURSE Chocolate Pecan Brownie Served warm with homemade vanilla ice cream. Pairing – Strawberry Harvest	**IV COURSE** House Smoked Pork Chop with Turbodog Braised Collard Greens and Bacon Lardon and Shallot Demi Glace Pairing – Restoration Ale	**IV COURSE** White Chocolate Mousse Crêpe Cake topped with Orange Glazed Ponchatoula Strawberries Pairing – Strawberry Harvest	**IV COURSE** Chocolate Bread Pudding with Abita Turbodog Glaze Pairing – Turbodog
	V COURSE Strawberry Pound Cake with Abita Root Beer Syrup Pairing – Strawberry Harvest		

RECIPES

STARTERS... 55

SEAFOOD.. 85

MAINS.. 105

SIDES.. 143

DESSERTS... 153

HOW TO COOK WITH ABITA BEER

Beer has been around for thousands of years. Not only has it been a popular beverage, but it also has been used in cooking – to tenderize, to marinate, to braise, to bake, and to add a distinctive flavor to a variety of foods. When cooking with beer, it's only natural that some goes into the recipe and some goes into the chef as well. Everybody wins!

The primary ingredients used in brewing beer – hops, yeast and malt – are healthy and provide an incredible range of usage. At one time, beer was referred to as "liquid bread".

There are various beer styles, which are determined by the color, flavor, strength, ingredients, production method, recipe, history or origin. As an ingredient in cooking, beer enhances the flavor of certain foods depending on the style of the beer. Dark robust ales (think Abita Turbodog) are ideal for braising meats like pork and beef or for caramelizing onions for a French onion soup.

On the other hand, lighter lagers, such as Abita Amber and Abita Wheat, work best in cream-style soups, butter-based sauces and batters. Lighter-style beers work best when cooking most seafood – scallops, shrimp, crabmeat, fish, mussels and the like. Sweeter brews, such as Abita Strawberry Harvest Lager and Purple Haze, are ideal for making sweet custards, dessert sauces and sweet salad dressings. Sweet beers, when reduced to a syrupy consistency, make great glazes for pork and chicken. Abita Root Beer makes an outstanding glaze, too.

Many people choose to make a reduction sauce to enhance the flavor of their dish. By reducing the cooking liquid down using heat, you are able to concentrate the flavor profile of the reduced ingredient. This process can be used when cooking with your favorite Abita Beers. For example, a

reduction sauce of Purple Haze would be sweeter and the hop and bitter flavors found in Jockamo I.P.A. and Restoration Pale Ale would become even more pronounced.

Experiment when making baked goods such as biscuits and breads. Try making breads with different styles of beer until you determine the flavor you like best. The same goes for making pancake batters or batters used for frying.

Beer, especially Abita's Turbodog and Amber, make great marinades for meat (beef, lamb, chicken and pork) for the simple reason that they add distinctive flavors. Feel free to add other ingredients, such as onions, peppers, Worcestershire sauce, olive oil, fresh herbs, citrus juice and other seasonings to enhance the flavor even more.

Add the beer of your choice to the pot when making chili, stews and soups.

Try soaking fruit (especially berries, apples and pears) in beer, such as Abita Strawberry Harvest Lager or Purple Haze, to infuse it with the liquid's flavor. The macerated fruit can then be added to salads, cakes, puddings and breads.

Beer also can be used for poaching fish and chicken, making fondues, and steaming clams and vegetables. When cooking rice, substitute beer for the water or broth for an incredible flavor.

Rather than using wine, deglaze your pan with beer to make a delicious sauce or gravy to accompany the food cooked in the pan.

Have your own adventure in cooking and baking with beer! Experimenting is half the fun!

STARTERS

SOUPS, SALADS & SMALL BITES

COOKING LOUISIANA TRUE

CHAPTER No. 1

CEVICHE BEER SHOTS

CHEF PAUL CONWAY · GLORIOSA CATERING, ATLANTA, GEORGIA

6 SERVINGS | *suggested pairing:* RESTORATION ALE, GOLDEN *or* AMBER · *made with* AMBER

Chef Paul, a 1987 graduate of the Culinary Institute of America, and Gloriosa owner Keith Robinson produce events in Atlanta and around the country that are unparalleled in vision, style and culinary excellence.

INGREDIENTS

Make sure that all the seafood is very, very fresh!

1/2 pound shrimp, peeled and deveined
1/2 pound scallops
1/2 pound swordfish
1 cup freshly squeezed lime juice
1/3 cup rice wine vinegar
1 teaspoon minced garlic
1/2 cup finely chopped red bell peppers
1/2 cup finely chopped green bell peppers
1/2 cup finely chopped red onions
1 teaspoon Cajun spice seasoning
2 tablespoons granulated sugar
1/2 cup extra-virgin olive oil
1/2 cup chopped fresh cilantro
1 (12-ounce) bottle Abita Amber, divided

DIRECTIONS

Cut the shrimp, scallops and swordfish into medium to small pieces; put in a glass or plastic container.

Combine the lime juice, vinegar, garlic, bell peppers, onions, Cajun seasoning, sugar, oil and cilantro in a bowl and stir to mix. Pour the mixture over the seafood. Cover and refrigerate for 6 to 8 hours, stirring every hour.

When ready to serve, add half of the beer. Divide the seafood mixture among 6 or more shot glasses; pour a splash of the remaining beer over the seafood in each glass and serve immediately.

Discard any leftovers.

NOTE: FRESH seafood, such as tuna, salmon, redfish and sea bass, also can be used for this recipe. The acid from the limes and vinegar changes the structure of the proteins in the fish, essentially "cooking" the fish without using heat. If you have concerns about raw fish or seafood, lightly sauté the fish or seafood and refrigerate it before adding the marinade mixture.

ABITA TURBODOG
BARBECUED ALLIGATOR LEGS

CHEF GREG COLLIER · RALPH BRENNAN'S RED FISH GRILL, NEW ORLEANS, LOUISIANA

6 SERVINGS

suggested pairing: TURBODOG, JOCKAMO *or* FALL FEST · *made with* TURBODOG

An award-winning casual New Orleans seafood restaurant located at the gateway to the French Quarter at 115 Bourbon Street, Red Fish Grill sets the tone for your entire French Quarter experience.

INGREDIENTS

1 gallon water

1/4 cup kosher salt

1 medium onion, coarsely chopped

1 tablespoon liquid crab boil

2 tablespoons Creole seasoning

5 pounds alligator legs, skinned

BARBECUE SAUCE

1 tablespoon butter

1/2 medium onion, chopped

1 tablespoon minced garlic

3 ounces (3/8 cup) Abita Turbodog

9 ounces (1 1/8 cups) ketchup

1 tablespoon molasses

1 tablespoon Crystal hot sauce
(or other hot sauce)

3 tablespoons cider vinegar

6 tablespoons dark brown sugar

1/2 teaspoon kosher salt

1/2 teaspoon black pepper

DIRECTIONS

Combine the water, salt, onion, crab boil and Creole seasoning in a large, heavy pot over medium heat. Bring to a gentle boil. Add the alligator legs and simmer until the meat begins to fall off the bone. Drain. Pick the meat off the bones. Set aside.

Prepare Barbecue Sauce. While sauce is cooking, preheat the oven to 350 degrees. Toss alligator meat with barbecue sauce and arrange in a baking pan. Bake in 350-degree oven for 15 minutes. Serve warm.

NOTE: In Louisiana, some specialty markets and supermarkets carry alligator meat. Alligator legs and meat also are available at www.nafood.com.

BARBECUE SAUCE

Heat the butter in a saucepan over medium heat. Add the onion and garlic; cook, stirring until they are soft, 3 to 5 minutes. Add beer, ketchup, molasses, hot sauce, vinegar, brown sugar, salt and pepper. Simmer, stirring occasionally, until the mixture thickens, about 20 minutes. Transfer the mixture to an electric blender and puree. Use as directed in the directions above.

GOLDEN ABITA POMODORI WITH FRESH CRAB FINGERS

CHEF TERRY MCDONNER · JUBAN'S RESTAURANT, BATON ROUGE, LOUISIANA

4 SERVINGS — *suggested pairing:* GOLDEN, RESTORATION ALE *or* AMBER · *made with* GOLDEN

Acclaimed Creole cuisine, gracious hospitality and a relaxed atmosphere have been the hallmarks of Juban's since 1983.

INGREDIENTS

1/4 cup olive oil

3 tablespoons unsalted butter

1 tablespoon fresh garlic, minced

1 pound fresh Louisiana crab fingers

8 ounces (1 cup) Abita Golden

1 pint teardrop tomatoes, cut into halves

1/2 cup thinly sliced fresh basil

Salt and pepper, to taste

Focaccia bread, for serving

DIRECTIONS

Combine the olive oil, butter and garlic in a large skillet over medium heat. Cook, stirring until fragrant, about 1-1/2 minutes, being careful not to burn the garlic.

Add the crab fingers and cook for 1 minute. Add the beer; stir to loosen any browned bits from bottom of pan. Add the tomato halves and cook until the liquid in the pan is reduced by half. Add the basil and stir gently. Season with salt and pepper.

Divide crab mixture among 4 warm bowls and serve with focaccia bread.

DRUNKEN MUSSELS

CHEF/OWNER JULIAN GAXHOLLI · BAYOU RESTAURANT, STATEN ISLAND, NEW YORK

1 SERVING	*suggested pairing:* AMBER, RESTORATION ALE *or* TURBODOG *made with* AMBER *or* TURBODOG

One of Staten Island's newest dining experiences is a Cajun-Creole taste of old New Orleans. A loving and award-winning New York re-creation of a Bourbon Street bistro with a menu inspired by the flavors of this distinctive American region. The Bayou Restaurant is where the "Big Easy" meets the "Big Apple".

INGREDIENTS

2 tablespoons extra-virgin olive oil

4 garlic cloves, cut into slivers

12 fresh mussels in the shell

6 ounces (3/4 cup) Abita Amber or Abita Turbodog

3 ounces canned clam juice

Pinch dried oregano

Pinch crushed red pepper

Pinch Cajun seasoning

1 tablespoon butter

2 flour tortillas

1 tablespoon chopped fresh cilantro

NOTE: When choosing fresh mussels, discard mussels with broken or open shells. Gently tap any shell that opens before cooking. If it does not close, throw it away. Also discard any mussels that do not open after they are cooked. Scrub the shells and remove any barnacles as well as the black fibrous "beard." Purge the mussels of sand and debris by placing them in a container filled with cold water for 20 minutes. Rinse under cool tap water to remove any remaining sand and dry with a towel before cooking.

DIRECTIONS

Heat the olive oil in a large pan over medium heat. Add the garlic and cook, stirring until the edges turn brown. Add the mussels and toss with the oil and garlic. Slowly add the beer and simmer for 2 minutes. Add the clam juice, oregano, crushed red pepper and Cajun seasoning; simmer for 2 minutes. Add the butter and swirl around.

Grill the tortillas. Fold tortillas in half. Place the mussels and sauce in a large serving bowl. Arrange the tortillas on the side of the dish for dunking. Garnish with cilantro.

ABITA BEER-BATTERED TEMPURA SOFT-SHELL CRABS

WITH PONZU DIPPING SAUCE

CHEF HOLLY GOETTING · CHARLEY G'S, LAFAYETTE, LOUISIANA

4 SERVINGS	*suggested pairing:* TURBODOG, BOCK *or* GOLDEN · *made with* AMBER

Charley G's menu focuses on Southern Louisiana seafood and is inspired by Chef Holly Goetting, named a 2005 Chef To Watch by Louisiana Cookin' magazine.

INGREDIENTS

1 cup all-purpose flour, plus more for dusting

1 (12-ounce) bottle Abita Amber, divided

4 soft-shell crabs (about 5 inches in size)

Milk, for soaking crabs

Peanut oil, for frying

Salt and pepper, to taste

Chopped fresh chives, for garnish

PONZU DIPPING SAUCE

1/2 cup mayonnaise

1/4 cup soy sauce

2 tablespoons rice wine vinegar

1-1/2 tablespoons fresh lime juice

1 tablespoon mirin (see note)

1 tablespoon sesame oil

DIRECTIONS

Put 1 cup flour in a mixing bowl and make a well in the center of the flour. Pour 1 cup of the beer into the well and whisk until the mixture is blended. Cover and set aside for 1 hour. Before using the batter, whisk in remaining beer, as necessary, for the batter to be thick like pancake batter.

Clean the soft-shell crabs by cutting across the face with a pair of kitchen shears. Remove the eye sockets and the lower mouth. Carefully lift up the apron and remove the gills. Gently rinse with cool water and pat dry.

Place the cleaned crabs in a shallow dish and add enough milk to cover. Let the crabs soak for 12 to 15 minutes.

Heat 3 inches of peanut oil to 350 degrees in a heavy pot or electric fryer. Remove the crabs, one at a time, from the milk, allowing excess milk to drain off. Season crabs with salt and pepper. Dust the crabs evenly with flour, then coat the crabs evenly with the batter, shaking off any excess.

Carefully lower the crabs into the hot oil and fry until golden brown, turning once, about 2 minutes per side. Transfer the crabs to paper towels to drain. Repeat the process with remaining crabs.

Arrange cooked crabs on plates. Garnish with chives. Serve immediately with Ponzu Dipping Sauce.

PONZU DIPPING SAUCE

Whisk the mayonnaise, soy sauce, vinegar, lime juice, mirin and sesame oil in a small bowl. Serve with Beer-Battered Tempura Soft-Shell Crabs.

NOTE: Mirin is a low-alcohol, sweet golden wine made from glutinous rice. It is available in many Asian markets as well as some supermarkets.

SECRETS TO SOFTSHELL CRABS

1. To clean soft-shell crabs, hold the crab in one hand, and using a pair of kitchen shears, cut off the front of the crab, about 1/2 inch behind the eyes and mouth. Squeeze out the contents of the sack located directly behind the cut you just made.

2. Lift one pointed end of the crab's outer shell; remove and discard the gills. Repeat on the other side.

3. Turn the crab over and snip off the small flap known as the apron. Rinse the entire crab well and pat dry. Once cleaned, crabs should be cooked or stored immediately.

Abita Beer-Battered Tempura Soft-Shell Crabs, page 62

Cheddar & Abita Amber Soup, page 66

CHEDDAR & ABITA AMBER SOUP

ERIN KYLES · BATON ROUGE, LOUISIANA

6-8 SERVINGS

suggested pairing: TURBODOG, JOCKAMO *or* AMBER · *made with* AMBER

INGREDIENTS

1/4 cup (4 tablespoons) unsalted butter

1 yellow onion, finely chopped

2 ribs celery, finely chopped

2 carrots, finely chopped

1/4 cup chopped fresh parsley

1 tablespoon snipped fresh chives

1/3 cup all-purpose flour

1-3/4 cups milk

1-3/4 cups chicken stock

1 (12-ounce) bottle Abita Amber

1 tablespoon Worcestershire sauce

1 teaspoon dry mustard

2-1/2 cups grated sharp Cheddar cheese
(or more, to taste)

Tony Chachere's Original Creole Seasoning, to taste

Cayenne pepper, to taste

DIRECTIONS

Melt the butter in a large, heavy pot over medium-low heat. Add the onion, celery and carrots. Cook, stirring occasionally, for about 10 minutes. Add the parsley and chives and cook for 5 minutes. Stir in the flour and cook, stirring, for 2 to 3 minutes. Increase the heat to medium-high. Whisk in the milk and chicken stock. Bring to a simmer and cook, stirring often, until the mixture thickens, 8 to 10 minutes.

Pour the mixture into an electric blender and puree until smooth.

Return the pureed mixture to the pot over medium heat. Add the beer, Worcestershire sauce and dry mustard. Simmer until the foam subsides, about 5 minutes.

Whisk in the cheese, 1/2 cup at a time, letting each addition melt before adding more. Do not allow the soup to boil. Season with Creole seasoning and cayenne. Serve immediately.

OYSTER SOUP PROVENCAL

CHEF BRIAN LANDRY · GALATOIRE'S RESTAURANT, NEW ORLEANS, LOUISIANA

16 SERVINGS	*suggested pairing:* AMBER, LIGHT *or* WHEAT · *made with* ABITA SELECT SAISON

The grand dame of New Orleans' old-line restaurants, Galatoire's has remained committed to culinary excellence for more than a century. Under the guidance of fourth-generation family ownership, time-honored customs still bind the renowned restaurant, most important of which is the rich tradition of serving authentic French Creole cuisine at a level that raises consistency to an art form.

INGREDIENTS

1 stick (1/2 cup) plus 2 tablespoons butter

1 cup all-purpose flour

1/2 gallon freshly shucked
Louisiana oysters and their liquor

3 tablespoons vegetable oil

3 cups chopped fennel bulb
(Florence fennel or finocchio)

2 cups chopped leeks

2 cups chopped yellow onions

5 red potatoes, diced

3/4 quart canned Roma tomatoes with juice

4 bay leaves

4 sprigs fresh thyme

1/2 teaspoon saffron

1/2 tablespoon salt

1/2 tablespoon black peppercorns

1 quart Abita Select Saison
(if Saison is not available, substitute
Abita Wheat with a squeeze of lemon
and a pinch of white pepper)

1 quart heavy cream

Saffron strands, for garnish

DIRECTIONS

Heat the butter in a saucepan over medium heat. Add the flour, one tablespoon at a time, whisking constantly until the mixture thickens into a ball. Set aside. Drain the oysters in a colander, reserving the oyster liquor. Set both aside.

Heat the oil in a large, heavy pot or Dutch oven over medium heat. Add the fennel, leeks, onions, potatoes, tomatoes with juice, bay leaves, thyme, saffron, salt and peppercorns. Cook, stirring, until the vegetables are soft and lightly golden, 6 to 8 minutes. Add the beer and bring to a gentle boil. Cook for 5 minutes. Add the oyster liquor. Add enough water to make about 1 gallon of liquid. Bring the soup to a boil, then reduce heat to medium-low. Simmer for 20 minutes.

Strain the soup through a medium-mesh strainer and return it to a clean pot. Add about 1 cup of the soup to the roux (butter-flour) mixture and whisk to blend. Add this mixture to the soup in the pot and whisk to blend. Bring the soup to a gentle simmer and cook 20 minutes.

Heat the cream in a saucepan. When it just comes to a simmer, add it to the soup. Strain soup through a medium-mesh strainer. Adjust seasoning. Add the oysters and cook until the edges begin to curl, 3 to 5 minutes.

Serve immediately, garnishing each serving with a few strands of saffron.

ABITA BLACK-EYED PEA VINAIGRETTE SALAD

CHEFS DONALD LINK & STEPHEN STRYJEWSKI · COCHON RESTAURANT, NEW ORLEANS, LA

6-8 SERVINGS	*suggested pairing:* RESTORATION ALE, AMBER *or* GOLDEN · *made with* AMBER

Chef/owner Donald Link and co-owner Chef Stephen Stryjewski, embracing the old-style traditions, receive whole pigs and oversee an in-house boucherie, creating boudin, andouille, smoked bacon and head cheese. Cochon is Cajun Southern cooking at its best.

INGREDIENTS

4 cups dried black-eyed peas
1/4 cup chopped fresh rosemary
10 garlic cloves
4 anchovy fillets
Zest and juice of 3 lemons
1/4 cup Abita Amber, divided
1/2 cup extra-virgin olive oil
1/4 cup Banyuls vinegar (see note)
2 tablespoons Cochon's Abita Beer Mustard
(see note)
Salt and pepper, to taste
Salad greens

DIRECTIONS

Soak the dried, black-eyed peas in water to cover for 4 hours. Drain the peas and place them in a large saucepan. Add water to cover by 2 inches. Bring to a boil. Reduce the heat to a simmer and cook until just tender, 20 to 30 minutes. Drain peas and transfer to a bowl to cool. You will need 4 cups cooked peas for this recipe.

With a mortar and pestle, crush the rosemary, garlic, anchovies and lemon zest. Add the lemon juice and 2 tablespoons of the beer. Slowly add the oil and whisk to emulsify. Add the vinegar and mustard. Season with salt and pepper. Adjust the consistency and flavor with remaining beer.

Toss the cooked black-eyed peas with the vinaigrette. Adjust the seasoning. Serve over your choice of salad greens.

NOTE: Banyuls vinegar is made from Banyuls sweet wine from a region of France that borders Spain. It is a more mellow vinegar than a typical red wine vinegar. Use it as you would any fine vinegar. If you are unable to find Banyuls vinegar, substitute a good-quality red wine vinegar.

Find Cochon's Abita Beer Mustard at cochonrestaurant.com or substitute any whole grain mustard.

BABY LETTUCES WITH PURPLE HAZE RASPBERRY BALSAMIC VINAIGRETTE

CHEF TERRY MCDONNER · JUBAN'S RESTAURANT, BATON ROUGE, LOUISIANA

4 SERVINGS

suggested pairing: PURPLE HAZE, WHEAT *or* RESTORATION ALE
made with PURPLE HAZE

INGREDIENTS

2 ounces (1/4 cup) Abita Purple Haze

2 tablespoons balsamic vinegar

2 tablespoons olive oil

Salt and pepper, to taste

6 ounces baby lettuces

1/2 pint fresh raspberries

1/2 cup honey-chipotle pecans

4 tablespoons white chocolate shavings

DIRECTIONS

Whisk together the beer, balsamic vinegar and olive oil in a mixing bowl. Season with salt and pepper.

Put the lettuces in a mixing bowl. Add enough vinaigrette to coat them evenly. Divide salad among 4 plates. Garnish with the raspberries, pecans and white chocolate shavings. Serve immediately.

ABITA WILD RICE & CHEESE SOUP

GIA SCIORTINO · METAIRIE, LOUISIANA

4 SERVINGS	*suggested pairing:* FALL FEST, TURBODOG *or* AMBER · *made with* TURBODOG

This is a rich soup that pairs well with a cold pint of Abita Amber, Fall Fest or Turbodog and warm crusty bread. Enjoy!

INGREDIENTS

2 cups shredded Cheddar cheese

4 teaspoons all-purpose flour

2 teaspoons margarine (or butter)

2 tablespoons finely chopped onion

1 (14-ounce) can reduced-sodium chicken broth

1 cup chopped apples (such as Braeburn)

1/2 cup cooked wild rice

1 (12-ounce) bottle Abita Amber or Turbodog

Ground white pepper, to taste

2/3 cup half-and-half

DIRECTIONS

Toss the cheese and flour together in a bowl; set aside. Heat the margarine in a large, heavy saucepan over medium heat. Add the onion and cook, stirring, until soft, about 3 minutes. Stir in the broth, apples, cooked wild rice, beer and white pepper. Bring the mixture to a boil. Reduce the heat to medium-low and simmer, uncovered, for 10 minutes.

Reduce heat to low. Slowly stir in floured cheese until melted. Add the half-and-half; stir to blend. Cook for 3 to 5 minutes. Serve warm.

ABITA BEER BREAD

CHERRY JOCHUM · BATON ROUGE, LOUISIANA

1 LOAF	*suggested pairing:* ANY ABITA BEER · *made with* ANY ABITA BEER

This is the very best bread-machine recipe. The beauty of it is you can use any Abita Beer product, fresh or leftover. My trick is to substitute beer for the 1 cup water called for in the original recipe. This recipe is tried and true. It is my family's favorite bread. Try this quick, delicious and easy recipe when you want fresh bread for any and every occasion.

INGREDIENTS

1 cup Abita Beer
(any type or seasonal, at room temperature)
1/2 tablespoon vegetable oil
1/8 cup (2 tablespoons) granulated sugar
3/4 teaspoon salt
2-3/4 cups all-purpose flour
1 package active dry yeast (2-1/4 teaspoons)

DIRECTIONS

Add the ingredients to the bread machine in the following order: beer, oil, sugar, salt, flour, yeast.

Use the recommended basic bread setting on any manufacturer's bread machine. If given the choice, you can select normal or dark. Always follow the manufacturer's instructions for making the bread in your bread machine.

ABITA BEER BISCUITS

CHAD OLIVARD · WYOMISSING, PENNSYLVANIA

1 DOZEN	*suggested pairing:* ANY ABITA BEER · *made with* GOLDEN *or* TURBODOG

Here's the recipe I use for beer biscuits. It's simple and perfect. I usually use Abita Golden or Turbodog, but any Abita Beer will do, and the flavor of the biscuit changes depending on which one you use.

INGREDIENTS

2 cups all-purpose flour
3 teaspoons baking powder
1 teaspoon salt
1/4 cup solid shortening
3/4 cup Abita Golden or Turbodog

DIRECTIONS

Preheat the oven to 450 degrees. Sift the flour, baking powder and salt into a large mixing bowl. Cut in shortening until mixture has a cornmeal consistency. Stir in the beer. Knead lightly.

Roll out the dough to 1/2 inch thickness. Cut with a biscuit cutter and place the biscuits on a lightly greased baking sheet. Bake in 450-degree oven until golden brown, 10 to 12 minutes. Serve hot.

WOOD GRILLED SHRIMP WITH LOUISIANA STRAWBERRY SALAD
& ABITA STRAWBERRY LAGER VINAIGRETTE

CHEF HOLLY GOETTING · CHARLEY G'S, LAFAYETTE, LOUISIANA

2 SERVINGS	*suggested pairing:* STRAWBERRY HARVEST, PURPLE HAZE *or* RESTORATION ALE *made with* STRAWBERRY HARVEST

INGREDIENTS

6 (8-inch) bamboo skewers
1/2 cup Abita Strawberry Harvest Lager
10 medium shrimp, peeled and deveined
6 Louisiana strawberries, quartered
2 tablespoons cottonseed oil
Salt and freshly ground black pepper
3 cups spring salad mix
3 ounces chevre (goat cheese)
2 tablespoons alfalfa sprouts
4 red onion rings

ABITA STRAWBERRY LAGER VINAIGRETTE
Makes about 3/4 cup
1 teaspoon dried thyme leaves
2 garlic cloves
1 tablespoon minced shallot
1/4 cup Abita Strawberry Harvest Lager
2 tablespoons balsamic vinegar
Salt and pepper, to taste
1/3 cup vegetable oil

ABITA STRAWBERRY LAGER VINAIGRETTE

Combine thyme, garlic, shallot, beer, vinegar, salt and pepper in an electric blender; blend until smooth. With the motor running, gradually add the oil through the hole in lid. The mixture will thicken slightly.

SHRIMP & LOUISIANA STRAWBERRY SALAD

Soak the bamboo skewers in beer for 20 minutes before using. Toss the shrimp and strawberries in the cottonseed oil and season with salt and pepper. Place shrimp on bamboo skewers and grill over wood fire until the shrimp turn pink and opaque, 2 to 4 minutes per side. Place strawberries on bamboo skewers and grill only until warmed, about 1 minute. Remove from skewers.

Toss the spring mix, goat cheese and strawberries with just enough of the vinaigrette to lightly coat. Arrange equal amounts of the salad mixture on two salad plates; top with equal amounts of the alfalfa sprouts, red onion rings and grilled shrimp. Or, re-skewer the shrimp and strawberries as kebabs for presentation. Sprinkle some of the remaining vinaigrette around the salad. Serve immediately.

ABITA BEER BATTER SEAFOOD BEIGNETS
WITH SAUCE AMERICAINE

KIM KRINGLIE CHEF/CO-OWNER · DAKOTA RESTAURANT, COVINGTON, LOUISIANA

8-10 SERVINGS | *suggested pairing:* AMBER, RESTORATION ALE *or* ANDYGATOR · *made with* AMBER

Dakota Restaurant has an eclectic menu that marries global flavors with the zing of Louisiana accents. Dakota's focus is on creating dishes that combine robust flavors and textures with the freshest products available.

INGREDIENTS

12 ounces fresh whitefish fillets,
cut into small cubes
4 ounces chopped peeled baby shrimp
4 ounces chopped peeled crawfish tails
4 ounces lump crabmeat
(picked for shell fragments)
1 egg, separated
2 tablespoons heavy cream
2 teaspoons fresh lemon juice
1/4 cup chopped green onions
2 teaspoons chopped fresh dill
2 tablespoons Zatarain's Creole Seasoning, divided
Vegetable oil, for frying
1 (12-ounce) bottle Abita Amber
3 cups self-rising flour, divided
1 egg

SAUCE AMERICANE
2 cups shrimp or lobster stock
1 tablespoon sherry
1 tablespoon brandy
2 tablespoons roux (equal portions of flour and
melted butter cooked together)
1/4 cup heavy cream
Salt, white pepper and cayenne pepper, to taste

DIRECTIONS

Place fish, shrimp, crawfish, crabmeat, egg yolk (reserve egg white for use in batter), cream and lemon juice in bowl of food processor. Puree until mixture has a smooth putty-like texture. Transfer mixture to a mixing bowl. Add green onions, dill and 1 tablespoon of the Creole seasoning; mix thoroughly. Form mixture into small (about 1 ounce) patties. You should have about 24 patties.

Preheat oil in a deep-fryer or Dutch oven to 350 degrees. Combine beer, 1 cup of the flour, egg and remaining 1 tablespoon Creole seasoning in a bowl; mix thoroughly. Whisk reserved egg white into batter. Place the remaining 2 cups flour in a shallow bowl. Gently dust patties with the flour, then drop patties into the batter; make sure patties are completely coated with batter. Shake off excess batter and carefully place patties in hot oil. (Insert patties into oil in direction away from you to avoid a serious burn.) Depending on the size of the fryer, cook 6 to 8 patties at a time. Fry for 3 minutes on each side, until golden brown. Remove the beignets from oil with a slotted spoon and place on paper towels to drain. Serve seafood beignets with Sauce Americaine (see recipe).

SAUCE AMERICANE

Combine stock, sherry and brandy in saucepan; simmer for 15 minutes. Add roux and stir continuously for 2 minutes. Add cream and simmer for 5 minutes. Season to taste with salt, white pepper and cayenne. Strain. Serve with Seafood Beignets.

ABITA BREW PUB CRAB FINGERS

ABITA BREW PUB · ABITA SPRINGS, LOUISIANA

2 SERVINGS	*suggested pairing:* TURBODOG, GOLDEN *or* AMBER · *made with* AMBER

The original home of the Abita Brewing Company more than 20 years ago, the Abita Brew Pub is nestled under the sprawling oaks in the heart of Abita Springs, near the historic Tourist Park and the Tammany Trace. View the original 15-barrel brewhouse and watch the cyclists and horseback riders from the patio or dining room while you enjoy lunch, dinner or an Abita at the bar.

INGREDIENTS

2 sticks (1 cup) butter

1/4 cup Worcestershire sauce

1 sprig fresh rosemary

2 tablespoons chopped garlic

1 pinch cayenne pepper

1 tablespoon black pepper

Juice of 1/2 lemon

1 pinch Creole seasoning

2 to 4 dashes Tabasco sauce

Paprika, to taste

1 pound crab fingers

4 ounces (1/2 cup) Abita Amber

French bread

DIRECTIONS

Combine butter, Worchestershire sauce, rosemary, garlic, cayenne, black pepper, lemon juice, Creole seasoning, Tabasco sauce and paprika in large skillet. Heat and stir until melted and well mixed.

Add crab fingers to seasoned butter; stir to coat crab with mixture. Stir in beer and simmer until crab is cooked and mixture is slightly reduced.

Serve with hot French bread for dipping in the sauce.

FRANK'S FANTASTIC
EASY-TO-BAKE BEER BREAD

KATHY TUJAGUE · ABITA BREWING COMPANY, ABITA SPRINGS, LOUISIANA

1 LOAF

suggested pairing: ANY ABITA BEER · *made with* AMBER

INGREDIENTS

3 cups self-rising flour
3 tablespoons granulated sugar
1 (12-ounce) bottle Abita Amber,
at room temperature
1 tablespoon butter, melted

DIRECTIONS

Preheat the oven to 375 degrees. Lightly oil and flour a 9x5x3-inch loaf pan.

Combine the flour, sugar and beer in a large mixing bowl. Mix well. Put the dough in the prepared loaf pan. Brush top of dough with melted butter. Cover with plastic wrap and let stand for 5 minutes.

Remove plastic wrap. Bake in 375-degree oven until brown and crusty, 40 to 45 minutes. Serve hot.

NOTE: After the bread has cooled completely, wrap it in plastic wrap and store in a cool place. Try toasting slices of the bread and serving it with your favorite jelly or preserves, or use it to make your favorite sandwich.

BEER HUSHPUPPIES

DENIS HERMECZ · SILVERHILL, ALABAMA

18 HUSHPUPPIES

suggested pairing: ANY ABITA BEER · *made with* AMBER

INGREDIENTS

2 eggs, beaten

2 tablespoons dry buttermilk powder

2 cups self-rising cornmeal

1/2 cup all-purpose flour

1 (12-ounce) bottle Abita Amber

1 large onion, diced fine

1 large green bell pepper, diced fine

Black pepper, to taste

2 tablespoons vegetable oil (use oil leftover from frying fish, if available)

Salt, to taste

DIRECTIONS

Put the eggs in a large bowl; beat well. Stir in the buttermilk powder. Add cornmeal and flour; mix well. Pour in about 1/2 cup of the beer. Stir and check the consistency; keep adding beer, a little at a time, and stirring until the consistency is thick yet pourable. Stir in the onion, green pepper and black pepper. Adjust the batter with more of the beer until the batter slides off the spoon.

Heat the oil in a large skillet (you can use the same skillet used to fry fish). Make sure the oil is hot; it should be about 360 degrees. Spoon the batter into the hot oil, about seven hushpuppies at a time. The batter will cool the oil faster than fish fillets do, so don't over fill the pan with hushpuppies. Fry for a minute on one side, then turn them over. When the hushpuppies are golden brown, remove them from the oil with a slotted spoon and place them on paper towels to drain. Season with salt immediately. Serve hot.

NOTE: For zestier hushpuppies, add chopped jalapeño pepper to the batter. Try dusting the cooked hushpuppies with a little paprika and/or a little hot pepper sauce. Many variations on this mix are feasible.

ABITA PURPLE HAZE
BARBECUE SAUCE

CHEF PAUL PRUDHOMME · K-PAUL'S LOUISIANA KITCHEN®, NEW ORLEANS, LA (© 2008)

2 QUARTS	*suggested pairing:* PURPLE HAZE, CHRISTMAS ALE *or* AMBER · *made with* PURPLE HAZE

In July 1979, Chef Paul Prudhomme opened K-Paul's Louisiana Kitchen® in the heart of the New Orleans French Quarter. In only a few years, Chef Paul propelled the distinctive cuisine of his native Louisiana into the international spotlight and continues to push the limits today by creating exciting, new American and international dishes with his own line of all natural herbs and spices, Chef Paul Prudhomme's Magic Seasoning Blends®.

Chef Paul is passionate about everything he does and his main goal is to make people happy and healthy through his food. "And always remember," he says, "Good Cooking, Good Eating, Good Loving!"

INGREDIENTS

1/4 cup vegetable oil

3 cups chopped onions

2 tablespoons minced garlic

4 tablespoons Chef Paul Prudhomme's Pork & Veal Magic® seasoning

2 (12-ounce) bottles Abita Purple Haze

3 cups tomato sauce (three 8-ounce cans)

1/4 cup Magic Pepper Sauce®

1 cup light molasses

1/2 cup Worcestershire sauce

1 cup distilled white vinegar

1/2 cup white wine vinegar

1/2 cup packed dark brown sugar

DIRECTIONS

Heat the vegetable oil in a 5-quart pot over high heat until almost smoking, about 4 minutes. Add the onions and garlic. Cook, stirring frequently, until they are soft, about 5 minutes. Add the Pork and Veal Magic seasoning and cook, stirring constantly, until the seasoning has darkened slightly, about 3 minutes. Add the beer and scrape the bottom of pot until any browned bits on the bottom have been loosened.

Add the tomato sauce, Magic Pepper Sauce, molasses, Worcestershire sauce, white vinegar, white wine vinegar and brown sugar. Reduce the heat to low and simmer until the sauce thickens, about 30 minutes. Use as barbecue sauce with grilled meats and poultry.

SEAFOOD

FISH & SHELLFISH

COOKING LOUISIANA TRUE

No. **2**

SAUTEED SNAPPER
WITH PECAN MEUNIERE
ACCOMPANIED BY MARCELLE'S RICE PILAF

CHEF BRIAN LANDRY · GALATOIRE'S RESTAURANT, NEW ORLEANS, LOUISIANA

6 SERVINGS | *suggested pairing:* AMBER, PECAN HARVEST *or* GOLDEN · *made with* AMBER

INGREDIENTS

3 cups pecan pieces
Meuniere Butter (see recipe)
6 boneless red snapper fillets, each 8 to 10 ounces
Salt and freshly ground black pepper, to taste
2 cups all-purpose flour
2 cups clarified butter (see note)
Lemon wedges, for garnish (optional)

MEUNIERE BUTTER - *makes 2 cups*
1 pound (4 sticks) salted butter
1 tablespoon fresh lemon juice
1 tablespoon red wine vinegar
1 tablespoon Worcestershire sauce

RICE PILAF - *6 servings*
Marcelle Bienvenu, St. Martinville, Louisiana
2 tablespoons butter
1/4 cup finely chopped yellow onions
1/4 cup finely chopped carrots
1 cup long-grain white rice, uncooked
2 cups Abita Amber
1 teaspoon salt
1/2 cup baby green peas
2 tablespoons finely chopped parsley

NOTE: For clarified butter, melt the butter slowly over low heat. Allow it to sit a bit to separate. Skim off the foam that rises to the top, and gently pour the butter off of the milk solids, which have settled to the bottom. One stick (8 tablespoons) of butter will produce about 6 tablespoons of clarified butter. Clarified butter has a higher smoke point than regular butter and is therefore preferred in some cooking applications, such as sautéing.

DIRECTIONS

Preheat the oven to 300 degrees. Arrange the pecan pieces in a single layer in a shallow baking pan. Toast the pecans in 300-degree oven until lightly browned, 10 to 15 minutes, opening the oven halfway to stir them while they cook. Remove from the oven and set aside to cool. While pecans are toasting, prepare the Meuniere Butter. Keep warm.

Season the fish with salt and pepper, and dust evenly with flour. Cover the bottom of a large skillet with clarified butter and place over medium-high heat. Shake any excess flour from the fish. Working with a few fillets at a time, place in skillet, skin-side down, and cook 4 to 5 minutes, then turn and cook other side, until a golden brown crust is formed. Add additional clarified butter as needed between batches. To serve, top each snapper fillet with equal amounts of the toasted pecans and warm Meuniere Butter. Garnish with lemon wedges.

If desired, serve with Rice Pilaf (see recipe).

MEUNIERE BUTTER

Melt the butter in a medium saucepan over medium heat, whisking constantly, for 8 to 10 minutes, until the solids in the butter turn dark brown and the liquid is a deep golden color. The butter should begin to smell nutty.

Remove the pan from the heat and continue to whisk slowly, adding the lemon juice, vinegar and Worcestershire sauce to the browned butter. The sauce will froth until the acids have evaporated. When the frothing subsides, the sauce is complete.

RICE PILAF

Preheat the oven to 350 degrees.

Melt the butter in a medium, oven-proof saucepan over medium heat. Add the onions and carrots, and cook, stirring, until the vegetables are just soft, 3 to 4 minutes. Add the rice and cook, stirring, for 1 minute. Add the beer and salt, and bring to a boil.

Remove the pan from the heat, cover with a tight-fitting lid and transfer to the 350-degree oven. Bake until the rice is tender and the liquid is absorbed, about 25 minutes.

Remove from the oven, stir in the peas and parsley and replace the cover. Let the rice sit for about 5 minutes, then fluff with a fork and serve.

Sautéed Snapper with Pecan Meuniere, page 86

New Orleans Barbecue Shrimp Shortcakes with Abita Amber Cream, page 90

NEW ORLEANS
BARBECUE SHRIMP SHORTCAKES
WITH ABITA AMBER CREAM

CHEF DANNY TRACE · CAFÉ ADELAIDE AND SWIZZLE STICK BAR, NEW ORLEANS, LOUISIANA

4 SERVINGS   *suggested pairing:* RESTORATION ALE, AMBER *or* WHEAT · *made with* AMBER

Café Adelaide and The Swizzle Stick Bar is dishing up a playful take on Creole cuisine with a side order of Big Easy bacchanalia served by the gracious hands of the new generation of the infamous Brennan clan. Inspired by the Brennans' beloved Aunt Adelaide, everything about Café Adelaide and The Swizzle Stick Bar is centered around her charming pursuit of the good life — from high-falutin' to low-down — with great New Orleans food.

INGREDIENTS

2 pounds medium shrimp, peeled and deveined

2 tablespoons minced garlic

2 tablespoons chopped fresh rosemary

1 tablespoon olive oil

Salt and pepper, to taste

1/3 cup Abita Amber

3 tablespoons Worcestershire sauce

3 tablespoons hot sauce

1 large lemon, quartered and juiced

1 stick (1/2 cup) cold unsalted butter, cut into chunks

Rosemary sprigs, for garnish

Lemon halves, for garnish

ROSEMARY & BUTTERMILK BISCUITS – *yields 12*

3 cups all-purpose flour

1 teaspoon salt

2 teaspoons granulated sugar

1 tablespoon baking powder

1 tablespoon chopped fresh rosemary

1 stick (1/2 cup) butter, cut into small pieces

3/4 cup buttermilk or more, as needed

1 teaspoon freshly ground black pepper

ABITA AMBER CREAM – *makes about 1 cup*

1 teaspoon butter

2 garlic cloves, minced

1 shallot, minced

2 cups heavy cream

1/3 cup Abita Amber

1/2 teaspoon cayenne pepper

Salt and white pepper, to taste

DIRECTIONS

Prepare Rosemary and Buttermilk Biscuits.

Prepare Abita Amber Cream.

Toss the shrimp with the garlic, rosemary, olive oil, salt and pepper in a large mixing bowl.

Heat a large skillet over high heat. Add the shrimp mixture and stir until the garlic is golden brown. Add the beer, Worcestershire sauce, hot sauce, lemon juice and lemon quarters; stir to loosen the browned bits in the pan. Cook, stirring, until the liquid reduces and is slightly thick, about 3 minutes.

Reduce heat to medium-low. Add the butter, one chunk at a time, allowing each piece of butter to melt before adding the next piece of butter and stirring constantly until all the butter is used and the sauce is slightly thick and glossy. Remove and discard the lemon quarters. Taste and adjust seasoning.

To serve, cut 4 of the Rosemary and Buttermilk Biscuits in half. Place each bottom half in the middle of an 8-inch shallow bowl and set the top halves aside. Pour the shrimp sauce over the bottom halves of the biscuits, dividing the shrimp equally among bowls. Place the top halves on top, to make four "shortcakes." Drizzle the Abita Amber Cream on top of each shortcake and around each bowl. Garnish with rosemary sprigs and lemon halves. Pass the remaining biscuits to use to sop up the sauce!

ROSEMARY & BUTTERMILK BISCUITS

Preheat the oven to 425 degrees. Sift the flour, salt, sugar and baking powder into a large mixing bowl. Add rosemary and mix well. Rub the butter into the flour mixture until the mixture resembles coarse meal. (There may be some pea-sized pieces of butter remaining.) Add the buttermilk and mix together without overworking the mixture. (If the dough is not moist enough, add more buttermilk, 1 tablespoon at a time, until the dough holds together.)

Roll out the dough on a lightly floured surface to 1 inch thickness. Cut with a 2-inch biscuit cutter. Place the biscuits on a parchment-lined baking sheet. Bake in 425-degree oven until golden brown, 15 to 20 minutes.

Use to assemble New Orleans Barbecue Shrimp Shortcakes or serve on their own to accompany any meal.

ABITA AMBER CREAM

Combine the butter, garlic and shallot in a medium saucepan over medium heat and cook, stirring, until shallot is just wilted, about 1 minute.

Reduce the heat to medium-low. Add the cream and beer; cook until reduced by half, 10 to 12 minutes. Adjust seasoning. Put through a fine strainer. Set aside and keep warm.

NOLA'S SHRIMP AND SMOKED CHEDDAR GRITS
WITH ABITA BEER-B-Q GLAZE

EMERIL LAGASSE · EMERIL'S FOOD OF LOVE PRODUCTIONS (© 2007), NEW ORLEANS, LA

8 SERVINGS

suggested pairing: LIGHT, FALL FEST *or* AMBER · *made with* AMBER

Chef Emeril Lagasse is the chef-proprietor of ten restaurants in New Orleans, Las Vegas, Orlando, Miami and Gulfport. The recognition and awards he has garnered have made him known to food-loving Americans everywhere. Emeril is an author, a television personality and the creator of cookware, cutlery and spice products. Chef Emeril received a doctoral degree from the highly respected Johnson and Wales University and practiced his art in several fine restaurants in New York, Boston and Philadelphia before heading south to New Orleans. Abita Beer is a favorite ingredient for Chef Emeril and his restaurants often host Abita Beer dinners.

INGREDIENTS

EMERIL'S ESSENCE SEASONING (see recipe)
SMOKED CREMINI MUSHROOMS (see recipe)
ABITA BEER-B-Q GLAZE (see recipe)
SMOKED CHEDDAR GRITS (see recipe)
CITRUS BEURRE BLANC (see recipe)
GRILLED GREEN ONIONS (see recipe)

1/2 pound bacon, diced
2 pounds medium shrimp, peeled and deveined
3/4 teaspoon salt
2 tablespoons olive oil
4 tablespoons butter, at room temperature, divided

DIRECTIONS

Prepare Emeril's Essence Seasoning, which is used in one of the secondary recipes as well as this main recipe. Prepare Smoked Cremini Mushrooms. Prepare Abita Beer-B-Q Glaze. Prepare Smoked Cheddar Grits. Prepare Citrus Beurre Blanc. Prepare Grilled Green Onions.

Place the bacon in a 10-inch skillet over medium-low heat. Render the fat from bacon until it is just beginning to get crispy, 10 to 12 minutes. Remove the bacon from the pan using a slotted spoon and transfer to paper towels to drain. Set aside until ready to use.

Combine the shrimp with 2-1/2 teaspoons Emeril's Essence Seasoning and salt in a large bowl; toss to blend. Set aside while you prepare the skillet. Place a 14-inch skillet over high heat. Add the olive oil and heat until very hot. Add 1 tablespoon of the butter to the skillet; swirl to melt. Add the shrimp mixture to the skillet, making sure that the shrimp are in one layer. Sear the shrimp until well caramelized on the first side, about 1 minute. Turn the shrimp over and add the bacon, Smoked Cremini Mushrooms and Abita Beer-B-Q Glaze to the skillet. Cook, stirring occasionally, until the shrimp are well coated with the sauce and just cooked through, about 3 minutes. Add the remaining 3 tablespoons butter to the pan and swirl until melted into the sauce.

When ready to serve, divide the Smoked Cheddar Grits among 8 entrée-sized shallow bowls. Drizzle about 2 tablespoons of the Citrus Beurre Blanc around the edge of the grits near the rim of each bowl. Divide the shrimp, mushrooms, bacon and sauce evenly among the bowls. Place a Grilled Green Onion on top of each serving. Serve immediately.

INGREDIENTS

SMOKED CREMINI MUSHROOMS

3/4 pound cremini mushrooms,
halved, or quartered if large
1-1/2 teaspoons Emeril's Essence Seasoning
(see recipe)
4 teaspoons olive oil

ABITA BEER-B-Q GLAZE – *makes about 1–1/4 cups*

1 cup ketchup
1 cup Abita Amber
6 tablespoons light brown sugar
1-1/2 teaspoons crushed red pepper

SMOKED CHEDDAR GRITS – *makes about 2 quarts*

6 cups water
Salt, to taste
1-1/2 cups quick-cooking or old-fashioned grits
(not instant!)
1 cup milk
1 cup heavy cream
4 tablespoons butter
6 ounces smoked white Cheddar cheese, grated
Freshly ground black pepper, to taste

EMERIL'S ESSENCE SEASONING – *makes about 2/3 cup*

2-1/2 tablespoons paprika
2 tablespoons salt
2 tablespoons garlic powder
1 tablespoon black pepper
1 tablespoon onion powder
1 tablespoon cayenne pepper
1 tablespoon dried leaf oregano
1 tablespoon dried thyme

CITRUS BEURRE BLANC – *makes about 1–1/4 cups*

1/2 cup freshly squeezed orange juice
1/2 cup dry white wine
1/4 cup freshly squeezed lemon juice
1/4 cup freshly squeezed lime juice
1/4 cup thinly sliced shallots
1 (2-inch) strip orange zest
1 (2-inch) strip lemon zest
1 (2-inch) strip lime zest
1 garlic clove, smashed
1/2 bay leaf
1 sprig fresh thyme
1/2 teaspoon salt
1/2 teaspoon black peppercorns
1/3 cup heavy cream
2 sticks (1 cup) cold unsalted butter, cubed

GRILLED GREEN ONIONS

8 green onions, root end and tips trimmed
4 teaspoons olive oil
1/2 teaspoon salt
1/4 teaspoon white pepper

SMOKED CREMINI MUSHROOMS

Combine the mushrooms, Essence and olive oil in a medium bowl. Toss to combine. Place on the rack of a stovetop smoker.

Prepare the smoker over medium-high heat using applewood smoking dust, or the smoke chips of your choice. When the smoker begins to smoke, close the lid. Smoke the mushrooms until cooked through, about 20 to 25 minutes. Remove from the smoker and set aside until ready to use.

ABITA BEER-B-Q GLAZE

Combine the ketchup, beer, brown sugar and crushed red pepper in a saucepan; bring to a boil. Reduce heat slightly and cook at a steady simmer until the sauce is translucent and reduces to a consistency thick enough to coat the back of a spoon, 5 to 10 minutes.

SMOKED CHEDDAR GRITS

Bring the water to a boil in a large, heavy saucepan. Add a generous teaspoon of salt and the grits, and stir with a wooden spoon to combine. When grits thicken, add the milk, cream and butter; return to a boil.

Reduce heat to a simmer, partly cover the saucepan, and cook for 45 minutes to one hour, until grits are very tender, smooth and creamy thick.

Add the Cheddar and black pepper; stir until cheese is melted. Serve hot.

CITRUS BEURRE BLANC

Place the orange juice, wine, lemon juice, lime juice, shallots, orange zest, lemon zest, lime zest, garlic, bay leaf, thyme, salt and peppercorns in a 1-quart saucepan and place over high heat. Bring to a boil and reduce until the liquid is nearly evaporated, 12 to 14 minutes. Add the heavy cream to the pan and reduce by half, 1 to 2 minutes.

Remove the pan from the heat and reduce the temperature to medium-low. Add a few cubes of the butter to the pan and use a whisk to stir constantly until the butter is melted. Return to the heat and add a few more cubes. Continue to place the pan on and off the heat, adding a few cubes of butter to the pan and whisking until all the butter is used.

Remove the sauce from the heat. Strain through a fine-mesh strainer. Keep warm until ready to serve. Do not allow the sauce to boil or it will separate.

GRILLED GREEN ONIONS

Place a grill pan over medium-high heat. Drizzle the green onions with the olive oil and season with salt and pepper.

Place the green onions on the grill and cook for 2 to 3 minutes, turning occasionally to ensure even browning. Remove the green onions from the heat and set aside.

EMERIL'S ESSENCE SEASONING

Combine paprika, salt, garlic powder, black pepper, onion powder, cayenne, oregano and thyme; mix thoroughly. Store in an airtight jar or container.

Use as an all-purpose seasoning in a variety of recipes.

BACCO CRAB CAKES
WITH TURBODOG CREOLE MUSTARD AIOLI

CHEF CHRIS MONTERO · BACCO, NEW ORLEANS, LOUISIANA

12 CAKES | *suggested pairing:* TURBODOG, RESTORATION ALE *or* AMBER · *made with* TURBODOG

INGREDIENTS

1 pound lump crabmeat,
picked over for shells and cartilage
1/2 pound crab claw meat,
picked over for shells and cartilage
2 tablespoons minced red bell pepper
2 tablespoons minced green bell pepper
1/2 tablespoon Creole mustard
1/2 tablespoon hot sauce
1/2 tablespoon Worcestershire sauce
1/2 teaspoon salt
1/3 cup mayonnaise
1 egg, lightly beaten
About 1/2 cup fine dry bread crumbs

FOR BREADING AND FRYING:
1 cup all-purpose flour seasoned with
1/2 teaspoon salt and
1/4 teaspoon cayenne pepper
Egg wash (1 egg beaten with 1 tablespoon water)
1-1/4 cups fine dry bread crumbs seasoned with
1/4 teaspoon salt, 1/8 teaspoon cayenne pepper
and 1/4 teaspoon paprika
1/2 cup clarified butter (see note on page 86)
3 tablespoons vegetable oil

TURBODOG CREOLE MUSTARD AIOLI (see recipe)

DIRECTIONS

Combine the lump and claw crabmeat with the bell peppers, mustard, hot sauce, Worcestershire sauce, salt, mayonnaise and egg. Gently mix well. Add enough bread crumbs (about 1/2 cup) to bind the mixture. Form into 12 patties and arrange on a baking sheet lined with parchment paper.

Cover lightly and refrigerate for at least 1 hour.

Put the seasoned flour in a shallow bowl. Put the egg wash in another shallow bowl. Put the seasoned bread crumbs in another shallow bowl.

Heat the clarified butter with the oil in a large skillet over medium heat.

Dredge the patties in the seasoned flour, then dip them in the egg wash, letting the excess drip off. Dredge the patties in the seasoned bread crumbs, coating them evenly. Fry the patties, 3 or 4 at a time, in the hot butter-oil mixture until golden, about 3 minutes on each side. Drain on paper towels.

Drizzle the crab cakes with the Turbodog Creole Mustard Aioli and serve warm.

INGREDIENTS

TURBODOG CREOLE MUSTARD AIOLI – *Makes 2 cups*

1/4 cup Abita Turbodog

2 tablespoons rice wine vinegar

2 tablespoons Creole mustard

2 egg yolks (see note)

1-1/2 cups vegetable oil

2 tablespoons minced shallots

2 tablespoons capers, drained

2 tablespoons minced fresh parsley

1/2 teaspoon salt

NOTE: Always buy fresh eggs from a reliable source. Do not use eggs past their expiration date or with broken shells. Small children, the elderly, or those who have health problems are advised to not eat anything made with raw eggs.

DIRECTIONS

Heat the beer in a small saucepan over medium heat; reduce by half. Remove from the heat and let cool completely.

Combine the reduced beer, vinegar, mustard and egg yolks in a food processor; process for about 15 seconds. With the motor running, slowly add the oil through the feed tube. The sauce will thicken.

Transfer the sauce to a bowl. Whisk in the shallots, capers, parsley and salt. If not using immediately, store in an airtight container in the refrigerator. It is best used within 24 hours because of the raw egg yolks.

Serve with Bacco Crab Cakes or with other fish or seafood dishes or as a dipping sauce for vegetables.

DELTA'S LOUISIANA BARBECUE SHRIMP WITH ABITA GOLDEN

CHEF IGNACIO CASTILLO · THE DELTA GRILL, NEW YORK, NEW YORK

4 SERVINGS	*suggested pairing:* GOLDEN, RESTORATION ALE *or* AMBER · *made with* GOLDEN

The Delta Grill is known for its down-home comfortable atmosphere and delicious food. Delta Grill owners Tom Burns and Tom Sullivan have created a classic Louisiana roadhouse eatery with superior food and a welcoming atmosphere.

INGREDIENTS

1 tablespoon margarine

20 large shrimp, peeled and deveined

1 teaspoon chopped garlic

1 teaspoon chopped fresh rosemary

1/2 teaspoon ground black pepper

1 teaspoon Chef Paul Prudhomme's Seafood Magic® seasoning

1 cup chicken stock

3 tablespoons unsalted butter

1 cup Abita Golden

1/2 cup Worcestershire sauce

DIRECTIONS

Melt the margarine in a large, heavy skillet over medium-high heat. Add the shrimp. Add each ingredient one at a time, mixing after each addition: garlic, rosemary, pepper, Seafood Magic® seasoning, stock, butter, beer and Worcestershire sauce. Reduce heat to a simmer; cook at a slow bubble for 3 to 5 minutes. Remove from heat. The shrimp will cook quickly and turn a pink color.

Serve 5 shrimp for each portion. Serve with white rice and top with extra sauce.

BLACKENED REDFISH
WITH ABITA AMBER BRAISED CABBAGE & BARBECUED OYSTERS

CHEF GREG COLLIER · RALPH BRENNAN'S RED FISH GRILL, NEW ORLEANS, LOUISIANA

6 SERVINGS | *suggested pairing:* RESTORATION ALE, AMBER *or* RED ALE · *made with* AMBER

INGREDIENTS

BEER-BRAISED CABBAGE

1/4 cup butter

1 cup finely chopped yellow onions

1 (12-ounce) bottle Abita Amber

6 tablespoons cider vinegar

2 tablespoons granulated sugar

1 medium head green cabbage,
cored and thinly sliced

1 teaspoon chopped fresh thyme leaves

1 pinch kosher salt

1 pinch black pepper

3 carrots, cut in matchstick pieces

BARBECUED OYSTERS

6 ounces (3/4 cup) Crystal hot sauce
(or hot sauce of your choice)

2 tablespoons honey

1/2 cup clarified butter (see note on page 86),
heated to 140 degrees

Vegetable oil, for deep-frying

30 freshly shucked oysters,
drained and patted dry

1 cup all-purpose flour seasoned
with salt and pepper

BLACKENED REDFISH

6 redfish fillets, each 7 to 8 ounces

1/4 cup vegetable oil

2 tablespoons Creole seasoning

BEER-BRAISED CABBAGE

Heat the butter in a large, heavy pot over medium-high heat. Add the onions and cook, stirring, until soft, 3 to 5 minutes. Add the beer, vinegar and sugar; bring to a gentle boil. Add the cabbage, thyme, salt and pepper. Cover and simmer, stirring occasionally, until the cabbage is tender, about 20 minutes. Add the carrots; cover and remove from the heat. Let stand for 5 minutes before serving.

BARBECUED OYSTERS

Combine the hot sauce and honey in an electric blender. Pulse once or twice to blend. With the motor running, gradually add the clarified butter. Transfer the barbecue sauce to a small saucepan and keep warm over very low heat.

Heat the oil to 350 degrees in a heavy, deep pot or an electric fryer.

Dust the oysters evenly with the seasoned flour. Fry, in batches, until golden brown, 2 to 3 minutes. Drain on paper towels and keep warm.

When ready to serve, toss the warm oysters with the warm barbecue sauce.

BLACKENED REDFISH

For the blackened fish, place a large cast-iron skillet over medium-high heat until it is very hot. Brush the fillets evenly with the oil and season both sides with the Creole seasoning. Place the fillets, skin-side up, in the hot skillet and cook until the seasoning caramelizes, about 4 minutes on each side.

When ready to serve, arrange equal portions of the Beer-Braised Cabbage in the center of six dinner plates. Place a fish fillet on top of each portion of cabbage. Top each fish fillet with five Barbecued Oysters. Serve immediately.

BARBECUE SHRIMP, ABITA STYLE

KATHY TUJAGUE · ABITA BREWING COMPANY, ABITA SPRINGS, LOUISIANA

2-4 SERVINGS | *suggested pairing:* RESTORATION ALE, TURBODOG *or* AMBER · *made with* TURBODOG

INGREDIENTS

3 sticks (1-1/2 cups) butter

1/2 cup extra-virgin olive oil

3 tablespoons dried onion flakes

3 tablespoons garlic powder

1 teaspoon ground cloves

1-1/2 teaspoons cayenne pepper

1 tablespoon black pepper

3 tablespoons barbecue spice

4 teaspoons paprika

2 teaspoons dried rosemary leaves

1/4 cup Worcestershire sauce

Juice of 1 lemon

2 bay leaves

1 (12-ounce) bottle Abita Turbodog,

at room temperature

2 teaspoons salt

5 pounds large shrimp,

heads on and unpeeled

DIRECTIONS

Preheat the oven to 300 degrees. While the oven is heating, combine the butter and olive oil in a baking pan large enough to accommodate the shrimp (use two pans, if necessary). Place the pan in the oven to allow the butter and oil to melt and blend. Watch closely so the mixture does not burn.

Remove the pan from the oven. Add the onion flakes, garlic powder, cloves, cayenne, black pepper, barbecue spice, paprika, rosemary, Worcestershire sauce, lemon juice and bay leaves. Stir to mix. Slowly add the beer and stir until the foam subsides. Add the salt. Set the mixture aside to allow the flavors to marry, 10 to 15 minutes.

Add the shrimp and stir to coat with mixture. Place pan, uncovered, in 300-degree oven, and bake, basting well every 10 minutes, for about 40 minutes. When there is a slight air space along the back of the shrimp and the shell has pulled away from the shrimp meat, they're ready!

Serve the shrimp in a large soup bowl with some of the sauce, accompanied by your favorite Abita beer and hot, crusty French bread.

SUSAN SPICER'S CRAYFISH CURRY

CHEF SUSAN SPICER · BAYONA RESTAURANT, NEW ORLEANS, LOUISIANA

4-12 SERVINGS

suggested pairing: WHEAT, AMBER *or* RESTORATION ALE · *made with* WHEAT

INGREDIENTS

1/4 cup peanut oil, divided

1 medium yellow onion, chopped

1 medium red bell pepper, chopped

1 medium green bell pepper, chopped

1 teaspoon finely chopped garlic

3 tablespoons all-purpose flour

2 cups shrimp stock

2 cups Abita Wheat

3/4 cup pineapple juice

2 tablespoons mild or hot curry paste

2 zucchini, diced

1 green apple, cored, peeled and diced

1 pound peeled crawfish tails or shrimp, deveined

Salt, cayenne pepper and red chili paste, to taste

Cooked basmati rice, for serving

DIRECTIONS

Heat 3 tablespoons of the oil in a large, heavy saucepan over medium heat. Add the onions, peppers and garlic and cook, stirring, until they are soft and golden, 5 to 10 minutes.

Sprinkle the mixture with the flour and cook, stirring, for 2 minutes. Whisk in the stock, beer, pineapple juice and curry paste. Bring the mixture to a boil, whisking constantly. Reduce the heat to medium-low and simmer until the sauce thickens, 15 to 20 minutes.

Shortly before serving, heat the remaining 1 tablespoon oil in a large skillet over medium heat. Add the zucchini, apple and crawfish or shrimp and cook, stirring, for 3 minutes. Add the mixture to the curry base and simmer for 5 minutes.

Season with salt and cayenne and add a bit of red chili paste to taste. Serve hot with basmati rice and your choice of suggested condiments. Recipe makes 4 entrée or 12 appetizer size servings.

SUGGESTED CONDIMENTS: crispy fried onions, chopped nuts, chutney, chopped egg, toasted coconut, lime pickle and poppadums (thin Indian wafers).

The name "crawfish" or "crayfish" comes from the Old French word écrevisse, which is rooted in the word crawl. Thomas Say, the first American zoologist to study these animals, first used the name "crawfish" in 1817. The English scientist, Thomas Huxley, coined "crayfish" about 50 years later. Other common names include crawdad, mudbug and yabby. In the Eastern U.S., "crayfish" is more common in the north, while "crawdad" is heard more in central and western regions, and "crawfish" further south.

MAINS

MEATS, POULTRY & OTHER ENTRÉES

COOKING LOUISIANA TRUE

REALLY GOOD GUMBO

MEGAN HARRIS · MANDEVILLE, LOUISIANA

12 SERVINGS

suggested pairing: JOCKAMO, AMBER *or* GOLDEN · *made with* AMBER

INGREDIENTS

1 chicken, 2-1/2 to 3 pounds

1 pound fresh okra, cut crosswise into circles

3 tablespoons ground dried sage

3 tablespoons chicken bouillon granules

1/2 teaspoon dried oregano

1/2 teaspoon black pepper

2 pounds Andouille sausage

1/2 cup all-purpose flour

4 green bell peppers, chopped

3 pounds shrimp, peeled and deveined

1 pound crawfish tails, peeled

1 cup Abita Amber

1/2 teaspoon filé powder

Cooked rice

DIRECTIONS

Put chicken, okra, sage, bouillon granules, oregano and black pepper in a large stockpot; add water to cover by 2 inches. Bring to a boil; cook until chicken is done. Remove chicken and set aside to cool, leaving the chicken stock and okra in the pot. When chicken is cool enough to handle, bone chicken and shred the meat.

Fry the crumbled sausage in a heavy skillet until done. Remove sausage from skillet and set aside. Drain fat from skillet, leaving 1/2 cup of the drippings in skillet. Heat the drippings over very low heat. Gradually sprinkle the flour over the fat and immediately begin stirring. Stir the mixture constantly until it reaches a dark brown color, which may take up to 30 minutes. Remove from heat and continue stirring until it has cooled down a bit and there's no risk of burning. Add the sausage and the roux to the chicken stock mixture in pot and simmer 10 minutes.

Add bell peppers to pot; simmer 10 minutes. Add shrimp, crawfish tails and beer; simmer 15 minutes. Add the shredded chicken and filé powder to the pot; bring to a boil. (If time allows, let the gumbo rest for a few hours so the flavors will blend. Reheat before serving.) Serve over hot cooked rice, with crackers.

ABITA AMBER PULLED PORK

CHEF DARIN NESBIT · BOURBON HOUSE SEAFOOD & OYSTER BAR, NEW ORLEANS, LA

8-10 SERVINGS   *suggested pairing:* JOCKAMO, ABBEY ALE *or* FALL FEST · *made with* AMBER

INGREDIENTS

3/4 cup Creole seasoning

1/4 cup light brown sugar

1 pork picnic shoulder, 5 to 6 pounds (see note)

2 white onions, chopped (about 4 cups)

2 carrots, chopped (about 1 cup)

1 cup minced garlic

2 (12-ounce) bottles Abita Amber

1 cup tomato paste

2 cups Creole mustard

1 cup Steen's 100% Pure Cane Syrup

1 cup Steen's Cane Vinegar

1/2 cup Tabasco® Chipotle Pepper Sauce

1 cup Worcestershire sauce

1 quart chicken or pork stock

NOTE: Pork picnic shoulder is also known as pork arm picnic, pork picnic roast, fresh pork picnic, pork picnic shoulder roast or fresh pork picnic ham. Southerners like to use this fatty, bony cut to make barbecued pulled pork. It's also available boneless. This is also a good, economical cut to get if you want to make ground pork, kabobs or stir-fry strips. You can substitute Boston butt (similar, but with a slightly different flavor).

DIRECTIONS

Combine the Creole seasoning and brown sugar in a bowl and mix well. Coat the pork shoulder with the mixture. Wrap securely in plastic wrap and refrigerate for at least 8 hours. Preheat the oven to 250 degrees. Unwrap the shoulder and discard wrappings. Sear meat evenly on all sides in a large roasting pan over high heat. Transfer pan to 250-degree oven and bake, uncovered, until the meat is falling off the bone, 5 to 6 hours.

Remove the roasting pan from the oven and transfer the shoulder to a platter. Set meat aside to cool. Put the roasting pan on two burners on the stovetop over medium heat. Add the onions, carrots and garlic to the drippings in the roasting pan. Cook, stirring, until the vegetables are soft, about 5 minutes. Add the beer and stir to loosen the bits in the bottom of the pan. Add the tomato paste, mustard, cane syrup, cane vinegar, chipotle pepper sauce, Worcestershire sauce and stock. Cook, stirring occasionally, until the mixture thickens, about 1 hour.

Remove the cooled pork from the bone. Shred pork and add to the mixture in the pan. Cook for 30 minutes. Serve on hamburger buns or po'boy loaf with coleslaw.

ANDOUILLE SAUSAGE

CHEFS DONALD LINK & STEPHEN STRYJEWSKI · COCHON RESTAURANT, NEW ORLEANS, LA

5 POUNDS | *suggested pairing:* FALL FEST, JOCKAMO *or* TURBODOG · *made with* AMBER

INGREDIENTS

5 pounds pork butt, cut into 1-inch cubes

1 pound pork fat, cut into 1-inch cubes

1 (12-ounce) bottle Abita Amber

4 ounces (about 1/2 cup) minced garlic

2 bay leaves, ground

1 tablespoon each dried rosemary, thyme, sage, crushed red pepper and chili powder

1/2 teaspoon smoked paprika (LaChinata brand preferred)

1/4 teaspoon ground white pepper

1/2 teaspoon cayenne pepper

1-1/2 teaspoons filé powder

2 tablespoons salt

1 tablespoon ground black pepper

44-millimeter hog casings or medium hog middles (see note)

1 (2-pound) bag hickory wood chips

1 (2-pound) bag pecan wood chips

NOTE: Hog casings are usually available at specialty meat markets and some supermarkets. They also are available on the Internet.

DIRECTIONS

Combine pork butt, pork fat, beer, garlic, bay leaves, rosemary, thyme, sage, crushed red pepper, chili powder, paprika, white pepper, cayenne, filé powder, salt and black pepper; mix well. Store in an airtight container and refrigerate for at least 8 hours to allow the ingredients to marry.

Grind half of the mixture with a meat grinder through a 1/3-inch die and the other half through a 1/4-inch die. Recombine the two mixtures and mix well to release any air pockets so that the mixture is dense and the ingredients are evenly mixed.

Cook a small patty of the mixture in a skillet to check the seasoning and adjust as needed.

Stuff the mixture into 44-millimeter hog casings or medium hog middles and let dry overnight (or as long as possible for a more intense flavor).

Smoke the sausages in a smoker heated to 160 degrees over the combined hickory and pecan wood chips. Over a 4-hour period, slowly raise the temperature to 250 degrees.

Store the smoked sausages in the refrigerator for up to two days. Or, wrap in double layers of plastic wrap and freeze for up to one month.

TURBODOG COCHON DE LAIT

EXECUTIVE CHEF TORY MCPHAIL · COMMANDER'S PALACE, NEW ORLEANS, LOUISIANA

10 SERVINGS · *suggested pairing:* TURBODOG, ABBEY ALE *or* AMBER · *made with* TURBODOG

A hidden jewel in the heart of New Orleans' Garden District, Commander's Palace is truly one of the finest dining experiences in the world. Commander's setting, with sounds that soothe the soul, sets the mood for an unparalleled culinary adventure.

INGREDIENTS

1 pork sirloin roast, about 5 pounds,
cut into 2-inch pieces
Salt and freshly ground black pepper, to taste
1/4 cup vegetable oil
2 medium onions, chopped
2 ribs celery, chopped
2 carrots, chopped
1 (14.5-ounce) can diced tomatoes, undrained
6 garlic cloves
4 bay leaves
1 tablespoon chopped fresh thyme leaves
1 tablespoon chopped fresh sage leaves
2 (12-ounce) bottles Abita Turbodog
1 quart pork or chicken stock
Blond roux (see note)

NOTE: A blond roux is usually made by melting butter over low heat, then adding equal amounts of flour (for example, 1/2 cup butter to 1/2 cup all-purpose flour). The mixture is whisked constantly for about 2 minutes to remove the taste of the uncooked flour. This mixture is then used to thicken a gravy.

DIRECTIONS

Season the pork with the salt and pepper. Heat the oil in a large, heavy pot or Dutch oven over medium-high heat. Add the pork and brown evenly on all sides. Transfer the pork to a platter and set aside.

Add the onions, celery, carrots, tomatoes and garlic to pot. Cook, stirring, until the vegetables are soft and caramelized, 10 to 12 minutes. Stir in the bay leaves, thyme and sage. Add the beer and stir to loosen any browned bits on the bottom of the pot.

Return the meat to the pot. Add stock. Bring mixture to a boil, then reduce heat to medium-low. Cook, covered, until the meat is very tender, 1-1/2 to 2 hours.

Remove meat and set aside. Strain remaining mixture. Thicken the strained sauce slightly with the blond roux. Return mixture to a boil and return meat to the pot; cook until the meat falls apart and shreds easily. Season to taste with salt and pepper.

Serve over Louisiana popcorn rice or on French bread as a delicious po'boy.

Commander's Palace has been honored with the James Beard Foundation Lifetime Outstanding Restaurant Award. Deemed "the Oscars of the food world" by Time magazine, the Beard Awards are the highest honor for food and beverage professionals working in North America.

RESTORATION ALE WILD MUSHROOM & GOAT CHEESE TART

CHEF DARIN NESBIT · BOURBON HOUSE SEAFOOD & OYSTER BAR, NEW ORLEANS, LA

8 SERVINGS	*suggested pairing:* FALL FEST, RESTORATION ALE *or* AMBER *made with* RESTORATION ALE

INGREDIENTS

2 tablespoons unsalted butter

2 tablespoons olive oil

2 pounds assorted wild mushrooms, such as chanterelles, oysters, shitakes and cremini, wiped clean and sliced

1 medium Vidalia onion, thinly sliced (about 1 cup)

6 ounces (3/4 cup) Abita Restoration Pale Ale

1 cup (8 ounces) chèvre (goat cheese), softened

2 tablespoons assorted chopped fresh herbs, such as thyme, sage, basil and/or parsley

1 cup heavy cream

3 eggs, lightly beaten

Salt and freshly ground black pepper, to taste

1 (9-inch) unbaked pie shell

4 cups frisée, for salad

WARM TASSO VINAIGRETTE - *Makes 1-1/2 cups*

1 tablespoon vegetable oil

8 ounces tasso, finely chopped

1 large shallot, chopped

1 tablespoon dark brown sugar

1/2 tablespoon Creole mustard

3 tablespoons Steen's Cane Vinegar

6 tablespoons olive oil

DIRECTIONS

Preheat the oven to 450 degrees. Heat the butter and oil over medium heat in a large saucepan. Add the mushrooms and onion; cook, stirring, until the mushrooms are soft, 2 to 3 minutes. Add the ale and stir to loosen any bits on the bottom of the pan. Cook until all liquid is evaporated, 10 to 12 minutes. Remove from heat and transfer the mixture to a mixing bowl. Let cool slightly, then fold the chèvre and herbs into mushroom mixture.

Combine the cream and eggs in a small bowl and whisk to blend. Season with salt and pepper. Add the egg mixture to mushroom mixture; stir to blend. Pour the mixture into the pie shell.

Bake in 450-degree oven for 10 minutes. Reduce the oven temperature to 300 degrees and bake for 30 minutes.

Remove from the oven and cut into wedges to serve warm with a salad of frisée tossed with Warm Tasso Vinaigrette.

WARM TASSO VINAIGRETTE

Heat the vegetable oil in a large skillet over medium heat. Add the tasso and shallot; cook, stirring, until the shallot is soft, about 2 minutes. Remove from the heat. Add the brown sugar and stir until the sugar dissolves.

When the mixture is cool, stir in the mustard and vinegar. Whisk in the olive oil until well mixed. Serve immediately.

NOTE: You will not need any salt and pepper because the tasso is usually highly seasoned.

TURBODOG SHORT RIBS

AGNES BELLET, EXECUTIVE CHEF · LOUIS XVI RESTAURANT, NEW ORLEANS, LOUISIANA

4 SERVINGS

suggested pairing: TURBODOG, JOCKAMO *or* BOCK · *made with* TURBODOG

INGREDIENTS

2 tablespoons vegetable oil

4 thick-cut, meaty beef short ribs,
about 2-1/2 pounds

Salt and freshly ground black pepper, to taste

2 tablespoons butter

1 large onion, thinly sliced

1 carrot, finely chopped

4 garlic cloves, chopped

1/4 cup (4 tablespoons) all-purpose flour

1 (12-ounce) bottle Abita Turbodog

1 quart veal stock or beef stock

2 sprigs fresh thyme

DIRECTIONS

Preheat the oven to 325 degrees. Heat the oil in a large, ovenproof pot or Dutch oven over medium-high heat. Season the ribs with salt and pepper. Add the ribs to the pot, browning evenly on all sides. Transfer the ribs to a platter and set aside.

Pour off all but 1 tablespoon of oil from the pot; add the butter and stir until melted. Add the onion and carrot; cook, stirring, for 3 minutes. Add the garlic and cook, stirring, for 1 minute. Add the flour and cook, stirring, for 1 minute. Deglaze the pot by pouring in the beer and stirring to loosen any browned bits in the bottom of the pan. Bring the mixture to a boil. Add the stock and thyme.

Return the ribs to the pot. Cover pot and place in 325 degree oven. Bake until the ribs are fork tender, about 2 hours.

Remove the pot from the oven. With a spatula or spoon, carefully remove the ribs from the sauce and set aside. Skim off the oil that has risen to the surface of the sauce. Taste the sauce for seasoning and add more salt or pepper, if needed. Remove and discard the thyme sprigs. Put the pot on a stove-top burner over medium-high heat and bring to a boil; cook until the liquid is slightly thick and reduces a bit, about 10 minutes.

Return the ribs to the pot and heat through before serving over mashed potatoes.

ABITA AMBER MARINATED STEAK

PATRICE LOMBARDO · BATON ROUGE, LOUISIANA

4-6 SERVINGS | *suggested pairing:* JOCKAMO, AMBER *or* TURBODOG · *made with* AMBER

INGREDIENTS

4 to 6 beef steaks (any cut,
such as rib-eyes or filets)
McCormick's Season All or
your favorite seasoning mix
1 (12-ounce) bottle Abita Amber
1/2 Vidalia or yellow onion, chopped
4 garlic cloves, chopped
3 tablespoons Worcestershire sauce
1 tablespoon yellow mustard
1/4 cup olive oil
1/4 cup brown sugar
2 limes, cut into wedges

DIRECTIONS

Season the steaks evenly on both sides with the seasoning mix. Put the steaks in a large resealable plastic bag. Add the beer, onion, garlic, Worcestershire sauce, mustard, olive oil and brown sugar. Squeeze the limes and add the juice as well as the wedges to the mixture in the bag. Seal the bag securely. Shake the bag to evenly distribute the marinade. Refrigerate for 6 to 8 hours, shaking the bag several times to evenly coat the steaks.

Remove the steaks from the refrigerator about 30 minutes before grilling. Drain and discard marinade.

For best results, prepare a charcoal fire so that the coals are hot and white. (You also can use a gas grill.) Grill the steaks according to desired doneness, flipping the steaks only once during the grilling time. Serve immediately.

ABITA POT ROAST

CHAD OLIVARD · WYOMISSING, PENNSYLVANIA

6 SERVINGS

suggested pairing: TURBODOG, CHRISTMAS ALE *or* AMBER · *made with* AMBER

INGREDIENTS

1 (4-pound) boneless beef chuck roast

Kosher salt, freshly ground black pepper and garlic powder, to taste

3 tablespoons vegetable oil

1 tablespoon all-purpose flour

1 onion, chopped

12 ounces fresh button mushrooms, sliced

4 to 5 garlic cloves, minced

1 (10.5-ounce) can condensed beef broth

1 (12-ounce) bottle Abita Amber

DIRECTIONS

Preheat the oven to 350 degrees.

Season the roast evenly with the salt, pepper and garlic powder. Heat the oil in a large, heavy pot (preferably cast-iron) over medium heat. Coat the roast evenly with the flour. Brown the roast evenly on all sides.

Transfer the roast to a platter and set aside. Pour off the excess oil from the pot, leaving about 1 tablespoon. Add the onion, mushrooms and garlic; cook, stirring, until the onions are soft, 3 to 4 minutes. Return roast to pot. Pour the beef broth and beer over roast. Season with salt and pepper. Bring the mixture to a boil. Cover pot and place in 350-degree oven. Bake, basting occasionally, until the roast is tender, about 3 hours.

Remove the pot from the oven. Let meat rest for a few minutes before slicing it to serve with the pan gravy.

FOOTBALL BRATS WITH ABITA BEER

DUSTY KLING · BATON ROUGE, LOUISIANA

2-4 SERVINGS	*suggested pairing:* TURBODOG, AMBER *or* FALL FEST · *made with* TURBODOG

INGREDIENTS

1 (19-ounce) package
Johnsonville Hot and Spicy Brats
2 to 3 (12-ounce) bottles Abita Turbodog,
depending on the size of your pot
1 (14-ounce) can purple sauerkraut,
rinsed and drained well
Creole mustard
Large kosher dills

DIRECTIONS

Using a fork or a sharp knife, puncture holes randomly in the bratwursts. Place the brats in a pot large enough to accommodate them easily. Add enough beer to cover them completely. Cover the pot and bring the beer to a boil, then reduce the heat to medium-low and simmer until the brats are plump and cooked through. Transfer the brats to a platter and set aside.

Reduce the remaining liquid in the pot to an almost syrupy consistency. Add the sauerkraut; mix well and heat through.

Put brats on serving plates; cover with sauerkraut mixture and serve with a dollop of mustard and a dill slice on the side. An ice cold bottle of Abita Amber washes this dish down perfectly!

Variations: Grill the brats over hot coals for a few minutes after simmering to give them a smoky flavor and firmer texture. Purple Haze can be substituted for/combined with Turbodog for sweeter flavor. Brats and sauerkraut can be served on po'boy bread for a great sandwich.

POPPY TOOKER'S CHICKEN ETOUFFEE

CHEF POPPY TOOKER · NEW ORLEANS, LOUISIANA

| 6 SERVINGS | *suggested pairing:* TURBODOG, RESTORATION ALE *or* AMBER · *made with* AMBER |

Poppy Tooker is a native New Orleanian, classically trained in the art of cooking. She's spent her life immersed in the vibrant colors and flavors of her hometown. Poppy brought the international Slow Food movement to New Orleans by founding the local chapter.

INGREDIENTS

6 chicken breasts (bone in, skin on, wing removed), 8 to 10 ounces each

Salt and pepper, to taste

1-1/4 cups all-purpose flour, divided

1 cup bacon drippings or oil, divided

1 medium onion, chopped

1 medium green bell pepper, seeded and chopped

3 ribs celery, chopped

2 (12-ounce) bottles Abita Amber

1 cup chicken broth

3 garlic cloves, minced

2 teaspoons dried thyme leaves

1 bay leaf

2 tablespoons hot sauce

NOTE: If desired, use boned, skinned chicken breasts, which can be added to the finished gravy and cooked until tender.

DIRECTIONS

Season the chicken with salt and pepper. Put 1/2 cup of the flour in a shallow bowl. Heat 1/2 cup of the bacon drippings or oil in a large skillet over medium heat. Dredge the chicken breasts in the flour and add to the skillet. Brown evenly on both sides, about 4 minutes per side. Transfer to a platter and set aside.

Combine the remaining 1/2 cup bacon drippings or oil with the remaining 3/4 cup flour in a large, heavy pot or Dutch oven over medium heat. Cook, stirring constantly, to make a dark brown roux, about 20 minutes. Add the onion and cook, stirring, until the onion caramelizes, 8 to 10 minutes. Add the bell pepper and celery; cook, stirring, until the vegetables are tender, 3 to 4 minutes. Add the beer, broth, garlic, thyme, bay leaf and hot sauce. Season with salt and pepper. Cook briskly for 10 minutes.

Add the chicken breasts and reduce the heat to a simmer. Cover and simmer until the chicken is very tender, 1 to 1-1/2 hours. Adjust seasoning to taste. Serve over a bed of cooked rice.

POPPY TOOKER'S
CREOLE CARBONNADES

CHEF POPPY TOOKER · NEW ORLEANS, LOUISIANA

| 6-8 SERVINGS | *suggested pairing:* JOCKAMO, AMBER *or* TURBODOG · *made with* TURBODOG |

INGREDIENTS

1/2 cup vegetable oil

1/2 cup all-purpose flour

Salt and pepper, to taste

2 pounds beef stew meat, cut into 2-inch cubes

2 onions, thinly sliced

1 (12-ounce) bottle Abita Turbodog plus 1 beer bottle filled with water

2 tablespoons demi-glace (or the commercial beef extract products Marmite or Bovril)

1/2 cup Creole mustard

8 to 10 slices stale French bread (see note)

4 Idaho potatoes, cut into 1/2-inch cubes and boiled until tender

DIRECTIONS

Heat the oil in a large, heavy pot or Dutch oven over medium-high heat. Put the flour in a shallow bowl and season with salt and pepper. Dredge the meat in the seasoned flour. Brown meat, in batches, in the hot oil. As the meat browns, transfer it to a platter and set aside.

Reduce the heat to medium and add the onions. Cook, stirring frequently, until the onions are translucent. Add the browned beef, beer, water and demi-glace. Bring to a simmer and cook gently until the meat is tender, 45 minutes to 1 hour, adding more beer or water if needed to make a nice, thick gravy.

Spread the Creole mustard on the French bread slices and place on top of the stew. Cover and cook until the bread breaks down to make a thick gravy.

Serve with the boiled potatoes.

NOTE: If you don't have stale or day-old French bread, you can toast the bread in a preheated 375-degree oven until lightly browned, 3 to 4 minutes.

DEEP-FRIED BEER-BRAISED SHORT RIBS PO'BOY

OWNER/CHEF JACQUES LEONARDI · JACQUES-IMO'S, NEW ORLEANS, LOUISIANA

8-10 SERVINGS	*suggested pairing:* TURBODOG, ANDYGATOR *or* AMBER *made with* TURBODOG & GOLDEN

Located in uptown New Orleans, Jacques-Imo's embraces and interprets the New Orleans funky psyche in a way that is fetching to both tourists and locals alike. One of the hottest food tickets in town, Jacques-Imo's is known for its eclectic mix of Creole and Cajun specialties, at reasonable prices. Its irrepressible owner/chef, Jacques Leonardi, holds court each night dressed in a white chef's jacket, shorts and Birkenstock clogs.

INGREDIENTS

1/4 cup vegetable oil

5 pounds beef short ribs

Salt and pepper, to taste

1 medium yellow onion, chopped

1 rib celery, chopped

1 carrot, chopped

6 garlic cloves, finely chopped

1 (12-ounce) bottle Abita Turbodog

1 quart beef stock

2 sprigs fresh thyme

1 bay leaf

2 cups chopped white button mushrooms

8 to 10 French bread pistolettes

Mayonnaise

1-1/2 cups all-purpose flour

6 ounces (3/4 cup) Abita Golden

2 tablespoons baking powder

4 eggs

Seasoned flour, for dredging

Vegetable oil, for deep-frying

DIRECTIONS

Preheat the oven to 300 degrees.

Heat the oil in a large, heavy pot or Dutch oven over medium-high heat. Season the ribs with salt and pepper. Add the ribs to the pot (in batches so as not to overcrowd) and brown evenly. Transfer the ribs to a platter and set aside. Add the onion, celery, carrot and garlic; cook, stirring, until well browned, 10 to 12 minutes. Add the Turbodog, beef stock, thyme and bay leaf. Bring to a boil. Return the ribs to the pot. Cover pot with foil or a heavy lid and place in 300-degree oven. Bake for 4 hours. Add the mushrooms and bake for 1 hour, or until the meat is falling off the bones.

Remove the ribs from the pot and let cool. Remove the meat from the bones. Discard the bones and cartilage. Skim the fat from the gravy in the roasting pot and discard fat. Reserve the gravy. Hollow out the pistolettes and dress with mayonnaise. Fill each pistolette with equal amounts of the rib meat. Combine the 1-1/2 cups flour, Golden beer, baking powder and eggs in a bowl; whisk to blend. Dredge the po'boys in flour seasoned with salt and pepper, then dip in the beer batter to coat evenly.

Heat the oil to 350 degrees in a deep-fryer. Drop the battered po'boys into the hot oil and fry until golden brown. Remove from the oil and drain well. Slice the po'boys in half, and serve with a bowl of the reserved gravy (reheated) for dipping.

ARROZ CON POLLO Y ABITA GOLDEN

CHEF ADOLFO GARCIA · RIOMAR, NEW ORLEANS, LOUISIANA

4-6 SERVINGS

suggested pairing: GOLDEN, BOCK *or* WHEAT · *made with* GOLDEN

RioMar, established in mid 2000, is the culmination of many years of cooking in New Orleans, New York, London and Madrid. It's a top-notch restaurant that selects the best of the catch from local waters and the rest of the world and prepares it in a manner that highlights the impeccable quality of the seafood.

INGREDIENTS

1 fryer chicken, about 3 pounds, cut into 8 pieces

Salt and pepper, to taste

6 tablespoons olive oil

1 onion, chopped (1-3/4 cups)

1 green bell pepper,
seeded and chopped (1-1/4 cups)

1 red bell pepper,
seeded and chopped (1-1/4 cups)

1/4 cup (4 tablespoons) sliced garlic

1 bunch green onions, chopped (1-1/4 cups)

6 Spanish chorizo sausages or
8 ounces Louisiana tasso, chopped

1 bay leaf

1 tablespoon dried oregano

1 (12-ounce) bottle Abita Golden

3/4 cup diced canned tomatoes

1 cup water or chicken stock

1-1/2 tablespoons salt

2 cups long-grain rice, uncooked

DIRECTIONS

Season the chicken with salt and pepper. Heat the oil in a large, heavy pot or Dutch oven over medium-high heat. Add the chicken and brown evenly. Transfer the chicken to a platter and set aside.

Add the onion, bell peppers, garlic, green onions, sausage or tasso, bay leaf and oregano to pot. Cook, stirring, for 4 minutes.

Return the chicken to the pot. Add the beer, tomatoes, water or stock, and salt. Bring to a gentle boil, reduce the heat to medium and cook for 30 minutes. Stir in the rice. Bring to a gentle boil. Cover the pot and reduce the heat to medium-low. Cook until the rice is tender and the chicken is cooked through, about 30 minutes. Adjust seasoning. Stir and serve hot.

ABITA AMBER BEER JERK CHICKEN

CHEF MICHAEL SICHEL · FORMERLY OF 7 ON FULTON, NEW ORLEANS, LOUISIANA

6 SERVINGS

suggested pairing: TURBODOG, JOCKAMO *or* AMBER · *made with* AMBER

7 on Fulton brings a new sense of style to the restaurant scene in the city's Warehouse District. While the menu draws much of its inspiration from New Orleans' legendary cuisine, the dishes reveal a distinctly modern sensibility, beautifully presented and filled with grand flavors.

Jerk chicken recipes vary from chef to chef, cook to cook, so feel free to add such spices as ground allspice, ground nutmeg, ground cinnamon or a bit of sugar to the seasoning mix, according to personal taste.

INGREDIENTS

1 medium onion, chopped

1 garlic clove, chopped

1 (2-inch) piece fresh ginger root, peeled and chopped

1 bunch green onions, chopped

1 bunch fresh thyme, chopped

2 Scotch bonnet or habanero peppers, seeded and chopped

3 teaspoons Tony Chachere's Original Creole Seasoning

1 tablespoon salt

1 teaspoon cayenne pepper

2 fryer chickens, about 3 pounds each, cut into serving pieces

1 (12-ounce) bottle Abita Amber

DIRECTIONS

Combine the onion, garlic, ginger, green onions, thyme, Scotch bonnets, Creole seasoning, salt and cayenne in a food processor. Puree the mixture until smooth.

Rub the marinade mixture evenly over the chicken pieces. Place in a large resealable plastic bag. Refrigerate for at least 8 hours, turning bag occasionally to distribute the marinade.

About 15 minutes before cooking time, preheat the oven to 350 degrees. Remove the chicken pieces from the bag and arrange in a large baking pan. Discard any marinade remaining in bag. Bake chicken in 350-degree oven, splashing with beer every 15 minutes, until cooked through, about 1 hour. Serve warm.

ABITA BRAISED DUCK
WITH CILANTRO RICE

MARCELLE BIENVENU · ST. MARTINVILLE, LOUISIANA

4 SERVINGS

suggested pairing: WHEAT, RESTORATION ALE *or* AMBER
made with AMBER & BOCK *or* GOLDEN

INGREDIENTS

1/4 cup fresh lemon juice
1/2 teaspoon ground cumin
1-1/4 teaspoons salt, divided
1/4 teaspoon freshly ground
black pepper, divided
1/4 teaspoon cayenne pepper, divided
1 (4-to-5-pound) domestic duck,
cut into serving pieces
1/4 cup olive oil
2 (12-ounce) bottles Abita Amber
1 cup Abita Bock or Abita Golden
2 cups long-grain rice, uncooked
1 cup finely chopped fresh cilantro
1 cup frozen small green peas,
thawed in hot tap water and drained

DIRECTIONS

Combine the lemon juice, cumin, 1/2 teaspoon of the salt, and a pinch of the black and cayenne peppers in a small bowl; whisk to blend. Rub the duck pieces evenly with the mixture and put them in a large plastic resealable bag. Refrigerate for 6 hours. Remove from the refrigerator 1 hour before cooking to allow the duck to come to room temperature.

Heat the oil in a large, heavy pot or Dutch oven over medium heat. Add the duck and brown evenly on all sides. Drain off and discard all but 2 tablespoons of the fat from the pot. Add the beers and bring to a boil over high heat, scraping the bottom of the pot to loosen any browned bits. Reduce heat to low, cover and simmer until the duck is fork-tender, 45 minutes to 1 hour.

Transfer the duck to a platter and keep warm.

Pour off the cooking liquid, strain it, then measure about 3-1/2 cups strained liquid. Discard any excess liquid. Return the 3-1/2 cups strained liquid to the pot and bring to a boil over medium-high heat. Add the rice and return to a gentle boil. Reduce the heat to low, cover the pot and simmer until the rice is tender and the liquid has been absorbed, about 20 minutes. Do not stir the rice while it is cooking.

When the rice is done, stir in the cilantro, peas and the remaining salt, black pepper and cayenne. Arrange the duck over the rice; cover and heat over low heat for about 5 minutes. Serve warm.

TURBODOG BRAISED OXTAILS

CHEF ADOLFO GARCIA · RIOMAR, NEW ORLEANS, LOUISIANA

6-8 SERVINGS	*suggested pairing:* PECAN HARVEST, ABBEY ALE *or* TURBODOG *made with* TURBODOG

INGREDIENTS

4 pounds oxtails, cut at joint and
trimmed of excess fat (see note)
2-1/2 teaspoons salt
1/4 cup plus 2 tablespoons olive oil, divided
2 medium yellow onions,
peeled and chopped (about 3 cups)
2 tablespoons tomato paste
10 garlic cloves, chopped (about 1/4 cup)
1 pinch ground nutmeg
1 bunch green onions, chopped
1 tablespoon chopped fresh thyme
1 bay leaf
3 whole allspice
1 stick cinnamon
2 (12-ounce) bottles Abita Turbodog
2 cups water
2 habanero peppers, seeded and chopped
(wear gloves when handling these peppers)

COCONUT RICE – *Makes 8 servings*
2 cups jasmine-scented, basmati or
white long-grain rice, uncooked
1 tablespoon butter
1 (14-ounce) can unsweetened coconut milk
(not cream of coconut)
1 cup water, chicken broth or Abita Amber
Salt, to taste

NOTE: Oxtails (which are really not from oxen, but rather from cows) are not difficult to find. However, if they are not available, substitute meaty veal or beef necks, beef short ribs or shanks.

DIRECTIONS

Preheat the oven to 350 degrees. Season the oxtails with the salt. Heat 1/4 cup of the oil in a large ovenproof pot or Dutch oven over medium heat. Add the oxtails and brown evenly on all sides. Transfer the oxtails to a large platter and set aside. Drain off any excess fat in the pot.

Add the remaining 2 tablespoons oil to the pot over medium heat. Add the onions, tomato paste, garlic, nutmeg, green onions and thyme. Cook, stirring, until the vegetables are soft and lightly golden, 4 to 5 minutes.

Tie the bay leaf, allspice and cinnamon in a square of cheesecloth to make a bouquet garni. Add the bouquet garni, beer, water, habaneros and oxtails to pot, and bring mixture to a boil.

Remove from the heat, cover and transfer the pot to 350-degree oven. Bake until the oxtails are very tender, about 1-1/2 hours. Remove and discard the bouquet garni.

Serve with Coconut Rice.

COCONUT RICE

Rinse the rice in cool water and drain well. Melt the butter in a medium saucepan over medium-high heat. Add the rice and cook, stirring, until it becomes opaque, 2 to 3 minutes. Add the coconut milk, water (or broth or beer) and salt; bring to a boil. Reduce the heat to medium-low, cover and simmer until the rice is tender, about 20 minutes. Remove from heat.

Let stand, covered, for about 5 minutes, then fluff the rice with a fork. Serve with Turbodog Braised Oxtails or other main courses.

GRILLED MARGARITA PIZZA

JAY CONNAUGHTON · COVINGTON, LOUISIANA

1 PIZZA

suggested pairing: LIGHT, RESTORATION ALE *or* AMBER
made with JOCKAMO & TURBODOG

INGREDIENTS

FOR THE GRILL (OPTIONAL)
2 to 3 cups wood chips
2 (12-ounce) bottles Abita Turbodog
Aluminum foil

FOR PIZZA
1 (12-ounce) can tomato paste
1 (12-ounce bottle) Jockamo I.P.A.
(or Abita of your choice)
1/4 cup quality honey
1/4 cup quality olive oil, divided
3 large cloves garlic, minced
1 small bunch fresh oregano, finely chopped
1 small bunch fresh thyme, finely chopped
1 store-bought 12-inch baked pizza crust (either
from the bread section or frozen and thawed)
1 (8-ounce) package fresh mozzarella balls in
water, drained and sliced into thin rounds
1 small bunch fresh basil, coarsely chopped
Vegetable, peanut or olive oil,
for greasing grill rack

FOR THE GRILL (OPTIONAL)

You can enhance the flavor of the grilled pizza by smoking wood chips on the fire. Put 2 to 3 cups of your favorite wood chips in a large bowl. Pour beer over wood chips to cover them. Let soak for a minimum of 20 minutes. Place a large sheet of aluminum foil flat on the counter. Drain the wood chips and place them in the center of the foil. Fold all four sides of foil together to form a pouch; fold to tightly seal the pouch. Using a paring or steak knife, cut 8 (1-inch) slits in the top of the foil pouch to allow the smoke to vent. Set aside while heating coals and preparing pizza.

FOR THE PIZZA

Combine tomato paste and beer in a small saucepan over medium heat; cook, stirring, until heated through. Stir in honey. Cook until reduced to desired thickness, about 20 minutes. If sauce becomes too thick, add additional beer to reach desired consistency.

Meanwhile, heat half of the olive oil in a small saucepan over medium-low heat. Add garlic; reduce heat to low. Slowly cook the garlic while the tomato sauce is reducing. Do not let the garlic brown, or it will become bitter. Add the garlic-olive oil mixture to the tomato sauce along with the oregano and thyme; stir to combine.

Remove pot from the heat and let cool slightly. Once the sauce has cooled a little, spoon the sauce onto the pizza crust, being careful to not add too much. Next, arrange the mozzarella slices over tomato sauce; sprinkle with basil.

Drizzle with the remaining 2 tablespoons olive oil.

Heat coals in charcoal grill to medium heat (you can hold your hand over the coals for about four seconds), then spread the coals into a thin, even layer. Place the pouch of wood chips (if using) directly on the coals prior to cooking pizza and allow a few minutes for the wood chips to heat and begin smoking.

Place pizza on an oiled grill rack. Cover grill and cook pizza for 5 minutes or until toppings are heated through and crust is crisp. Check often so that the bottom of the pizza doesn't burn.

NOTE: This recipe can be prepared indoors in the oven; just follow the pizza crust instructions for cooking in the oven. You can use your favorite pizza dough recipe and substitute Abita beer for the water. If you are using fresh or raw pizza dough on the grill, you will need to change the position of the coals. Rather than a thin, single layer of coals, mound the coals along the side of the grill for indirect cooking; the cooking time will be lengthened.

BEER–BRAISED RABBIT

MARCELLE BIENVENU · ST. MARTINVILLE, LOUISIANA

6-8 SERVINGS | *suggested pairing:* AMBER, CHRISTMAS ALE *or* TURBODOG · *made with* TURBODOG

INGREDIENTS

2 rabbits, each about 3 pounds,
cut into serving pieces
Salt, freshly ground black pepper
and cayenne pepper, to taste
2 tablespoons unsalted butter
3 tablespoons olive oil, or more, as needed
4 leeks, rinsed well in cold water and chopped
(white part only)
3 medium onions, chopped
3 carrots, scraped and chopped
2 garlic cloves, chopped
1-1/2 teaspoons dried thyme leaves
1 bay leaf
2 tablespoons all-purpose flour
2 cups chicken broth
1 (12-ounce) bottle Abita Turbodog

are soft and lightly golden, 10 to 12 minutes. Add the flour and stir to blend. Cook, stirring, to make a blond roux. Add the chicken broth and beer, stirring to loosen any browned bits in the bottom of the pot.

Return the rabbit to the pot and bring the mixture to a boil. Reduce the heat to medium-low, cover and simmer until the rabbit is tender, turning the pieces occasionally to cook evenly, about 1 hour and 15 minutes. Remove the rabbit from the pot and keep warm covered with foil.

Strain the cooking liquid through a sieve, pressing the solids to extract as much liquid as possible. Return the strained liquid to the pot and cook over medium-high heat until it reduces to about 2 cups.

Return the rabbit to the pot. Check and adjust seasonings. Simmer until the sauce is heated through and the rabbit is warm. Excellent served with long-grain white rice cooked in Abita Amber.

DIRECTIONS

Season the rabbit pieces with salt, black pepper and cayenne. Heat the butter and oil in a large, heavy pot or Dutch oven over medium heat. Add the rabbit, in batches, and brown evenly on all sides. (Add more oil, if needed.) Transfer the rabbit, as it cooks, to a platter and set aside.

Add the leeks, onions, carrots, garlic, thyme and bay leaf. Cover and cook, stirring occasionally, until the vegetables

NOTE: Domestic rabbits, usually already cut into serving pieces, are sometimes available at high-end supermarkets and some local groceries. These days just about anything is available on the Internet.

SHEPHERD'S PIE

CHEF PAUL PRUDHOMME · K-PAUL'S LOUISIANA KITCHEN®, NEW ORLEANS, LA (© 2008)

1 GOOD-SIZED PIE · *suggested pairing:* TURBODOG, CHRISTMAS ALE *or* AMBER · *made with* LIGHT

INGREDIENTS

1-1/2 pounds ground beef

2 cups chopped onions

1 cup chopped celery

2 tablespoons minced garlic

2 tablespoons Chef Paul Prudhomme's Meat Magic® seasoning

6 ounces (3/4 cup) Abita Light

1 teaspoon Worcestershire sauce

1 (8-ounce) can tomato sauce

1/2 of a 6-ounce can tomato paste (3/8 cup)

2 tablespoons dark brown sugar

2 tablespoons all-purpose flour

About 4 cups cooked mashed potatoes

NOTE: If you like, you can add grated cheese when preparing the mashed potatoes.

DIRECTIONS

Preheat the oven to 350 degrees.

Cook the ground beef in a nonstick skillet over medium heat, stirring frequently until the pink disappears. Remove meat from skillet and set aside.

Add the onions and cook, stirring frequently until the onions are brown on the edges, about 4 minutes. Add the celery and garlic; cook, stirring frequently, until the celery is slightly faded, about 2 minutes. Add the Meat Magic and stir well until the seasoning darkens, about 1 minute. Add the beer, Worcestershire sauce, tomato sauce, tomato paste and brown sugar. Bring to a boil and simmer until thick, about 10 minutes. Add the flour and stir until flour disappears. Remove from heat.

Stir the cooked ground beef into the mixture in skillet; mix well. Transfer to a baking dish large enough to hold the meat and topping. Top meat mixture with the mashed potatoes, spreading them evenly over the meat mixture. Bake in 350-degree oven until the top is golden brown and the pie is heated through, about 45 minutes to 1 hour.

ABITA PAN-ROASTED CHICKEN

EXECUTIVE CHEF GUS MARTIN · MURIEL'S JACKSON SQUARE, NEW ORLEANS, LOUISIANA

4 SERVINGS | *suggested pairing:* RESTORATION ALE, AMBER *or* PECAN HARVEST · *made with* AMBER

INGREDIENTS

1 (12-ounce) bottle Abita Amber
2 tablespoons olive oil, divided
2 teaspoons chopped garlic
1 tablespoon chopped fresh thyme
2 teaspoons kosher salt
1 teaspoon crushed red pepper
4 chicken halves, boned
1 cup chicken stock
1 tablespoon butter
Zest of 1 lemon
1/2 cup chopped fresh parsley

GRILLED VIDALIA ONION RELISH
2 pounds Vidalia onions, cut into 1/4-inch slices
2 tablespoons olive oil
1/4 cup cane vinegar
2 tablespoons brown sugar
1 teaspoon dry mustard (preferably Coleman's)
1 teaspoon kosher salt

DIRECTIONS

Combine beer, 1 tablespoon of the olive oil, garlic, thyme, salt and crushed red pepper in bowl; mix well. Put chicken pieces in large resealable plastic bag; pour in marinade. Seal bag and refrigerate for one hour, turning bag occasionally to thoroughly coat chicken with marinade.

Preheat the oven to 350 degrees. Heat remaining 1 tablespoon olive oil in a large, oven-proof skillet over medium heat. Remove chicken from bag; discard marinade. Place chicken pieces, skin-side down, in the skillet; cook until skin is golden and crisp, then turn chicken pieces over. Transfer skillet to 350-degree oven and bake for 10 to 12 minutes or until chicken is cooked.

Remove from oven. Transfer chicken from skillet to a platter. Add chicken stock to skillet and stir to loosen browned bits from bottom of pan. Bring mixture to a simmer; cook until reduced by half. Stir in butter, lemon zest and parsley.

Pour sauce over chicken. Serve Grilled Vidalia Onion Relish (see recipe) on the side.

GRILLED VIDALIA ONION RELISH

Preheat grill. Rub onions with olive oil. Place onions on grill and cook until almost tender. Meanwhile, combine cane vinegar, brown sugar, dry mustard and salt in a saucepan; bring to a boil. Add grilled onions and cook until tender.

Serve relish alongside Abita Pan-Roasted Chicken or with other poultry or meat dishes.

ABITA ROOT BEER GLAZED PORK TENDERLOIN
WITH TASSO-CABBAGE HASH

BOB IACOVONE, EXECUTIVE CHEF · RESTAURANT CUVÉE, NEW ORLEANS, LOUISIANA

6 SERVINGS	*suggested pairing:* JOCKAMO, FALL FEST *or* TURBODOG · *made with* ROOT BEER

The name "Cuvée" refers to the premium wine extracted from the first pressing of the grapes in France's Champagne region. Restaurant Cuvée's menus feature regional ingredients and are contemporary celebrations of the French and Spanish influences that have informed New Orleans gastronomy for more than two centuries.

INGREDIENTS

2 pork tenderloins

Salt and pepper, to taste

2 (12-ounce) bottles Abita Root Beer

Vegetable oil, for frying

3 Idaho potatoes, peeled, coarsely chopped

1/2 white onion, cut in matchstick pieces

1 red bell pepper, cut in matchstick pieces

8 ounces Tasso ham, chopped

1 head green cabbage, chopped

1 cup chopped fresh parsley

DIRECTIONS

Season the pork tenderloins with salt and pepper. Grill the tenderloins until done as desired.

Meanwhile, bring the root beer to a boil in a heavy saucepan over high heat; reduce heat to medium and simmer until reduced to a syrupy consistency.

Heat oil to 350 degrees in a deep-fryer. Carefully add the potatoes to oil and cook until crispy; you will probably need to do this in batches. Drain potatoes on paper towels.

Heat about a tablespoon of oil in a skillet. Add onion and bell pepper and cook, stirring, until caramelized. Add the Tasso and cabbage; cook 5 minutes. Add the cooked potatoes and parsley; cook 2 minutes. Season to taste with salt and pepper.

To serve, place a cup of the potato hash in the center of each of 6 large round plates. Slice the pork tenderloins into 6 portions; place one portion of pork over each serving of hash. Drizzle the root beer reduction over the pork.

JOCKAMO I.P.A.
SLOW BRAISED PORK MEAT PIE
WITH SPICY ONION MARMALADE

CHEF NATHAN WINOWICH · HOUSE OF BLUES FOUNDATION ROOM, NEW ORLEANS, LOUISIANA

12 SERVINGS | *suggested pairing:* ABBEY ALE, JOCKAMO *or* AMBER · *made with* JOCKAMO

The Foundation Room at the House of Blues is a members-only 50-seat dining room. Membership supports the nonprofit International House of Blues Foundation, promoting cultural understanding and creative expression through music and art. "My ambition is to deliver an impeccable and memorable dining experience with unique ingredients that result in dishes speaking for themselves," says Chef Nathan Winowich.

INGREDIENTS

5 pounds boneless pork shoulder

1/2 tablespoon kosher salt

2 tablespoons olive oil

2 cups chopped yellow onions

1/2 cup chopped carrots

1/2 cup chopped celery

1 tablespoon coarsely chopped garlic

1-1/2 quarts Abita Jockamo I.P.A.

3 teaspoons white pepper

2 teaspoons kosher salt

2 1/2 teaspoons Creole seasoning

2 teaspoons chopped fresh thyme

2 teaspoons hot pepper sauce

3/4 tablespoon Creole mustard

2 teaspoons Worcestershire sauce

1/2 teaspoon ground allspice

1 egg, beaten

1-1/2 tablespoons sour cream

1 small bunch green onions, minced

1-1/2 tablespoons bread crumbs

Pie Crust (see recipe)

Egg wash (1 egg beaten with 1 tablespoon water)

Chopped fresh parsley, for garnish (optional)

PIE CRUST

5 cups all-purpose flour

1 teaspoon salt

1/2 teaspoon baking powder

2 eggs, beaten

1 cup vegetable oil

2 teaspoons white or cider vinegar

1 cup cold water

About 2 tablespoons flour, for rolling dough

SPICY ONION MARMALADE

6 cups julienne-cut red onions

1/2 cup packed brown sugar

2 tablespoons sliced jalapeno peppers

1/2 teaspoon cayenne pepper

1/2 teaspoon ground nutmeg

1/2 teaspoon orange zest

1 cup dry red wine

1/4 cup water

1 tablespoon cane syrup

1 teaspoon salt

1 tablespoon powdered fruit pectin

DIRECTIONS
Preheat the oven to 300 degrees.

Cut pork shoulder into five even portions. Season meat with 1/2 tablespoon salt. Heat oil in a heavy-bottomed roasting pan over medium-high heat. Using tongs, add pork to the pan and evenly brown on all sides. Reduce heat to medium low. Add onions, carrots, celery and garlic to pan; cook and stir for 5 minutes. Slowly add beer to pan and stir to loosen browned bits on bottom of pan. Simmer 10 minutes.

Cover pan with aluminum foil and bake in 300-degree oven for 4 hours. Remove from oven and let cool, then refrigerate for one hour.

Meanwhile, prepare seasoning mixture by combining white pepper, 2 teaspoons salt, Creole seasoning, thyme, hot pepper sauce, mustard, Worcestershire sauce, allspice, egg, sour cream, green onions and bread crumbs; mix well.

Remove pork shoulder from pan. Shred meat by hand, then coarsely chop the meat until you can form it into a ball. Skim fat from the braising liquid and discard fat. Strain vegetables from braising liquid; coarsely chop vegetables. Reserve braising liquid.

Combine the chopped meat, the seasoning mixture, 1-1/2 tablespoons of the braising liquid and 2 tablespoons chopped vegetables from the braising liquid. Mix well. Check and adjust seasoning. Refrigerate until ready to assemble the pie.

Prepare dough for pie crust (see recipe) or substitute your favorite pie crust recipe or store-bought refrigerated pie crust.

> NOTE - Leftover braising liquid and vegetables can be frozen and added to soups or stews.

Preheat oven to 325 degrees. Roll out pie dough; it should be thin and even, but firm enough to not tear when filling is added. Cut the dough into 3-inch squares. Place the desired amount of meat filling in the center of each square. Brush the corners with a little egg wash; fold corner to corner, then seal edges by pressing with a fork. Repeat this process until you have completed the desired amount of meat pies. (Any leftover dough or filling can be frozen for up to one month.)

Place pies on a baking sheet lined with parchment paper, leaving space between pies. Bake in 325-degree oven for 12 to 15 minutes or until golden brown.

To serve, arrange meat pies on a tray. Top each pie with a dollop of Spicy Onion Marmalade (see recipe) and garnish with parsley, if desired.

PIE CRUST
Combine 5 cups flour, salt and baking powder in a large bowl; stir with a fork to mix well. Make a well in the center. Add eggs, oil and vinegar to well. Mix by hand until flaky crumbles of dough begin to form. Gradually add the cold water, working dough by hand until the dough begins to hold its shape.

Pat dough into a ball, cover with plastic wrap and refrigerate at least 25 minutes before rolling out. Sprinkle dough with additional flour (about 2 tablespoons) when rolling out, if needed to prevent sticking.

SPICY ONION MARMALADE
Cook onions in large skillet over medium heat until translucent. Add brown sugar and jalapenos; cook, stirring, for 2 minutes. Stir in cayenne, nutmeg, orange zest, wine, water, cane syrup and salt. Increase heat and simmer 10 minutes. Stir in pectin; cook for 2 minutes. Stir well. Refrigerate until serving time.

Serve with Pork Meat Pies or other main dishes.

SIDES

VEGETABLES & OTHER EXTRAS

COOKING LOUISIANA TRUE

BERNARD'S SOUTHERN COOKED GREENS

EMERIL LAGASSE · EMERIL'S FOOD OF LOVE PRODUCTIONS (© 2007), NEW ORLEANS, LA

4 SERVINGS	*suggested pairing:* RESTORATION ALE, JOCKAMO *or* AMBER · *made with* AMBER

As a teen, Bernard Carmouche was a dishwasher at Commander's Palace in New Orleans when he caught the eye of then-chef Emeril Lagasse. Emeril made a pact with Carmouche: Stay in school and I'll teach you everything you need to know about cooking. When Lagasse opened Emeril's, Carmouche joined the team, working his way up the ranks. Bernard interned with acclaimed chef Roger Verge at his Moulin de Mougins restaurant in France but always credits his passion for food to lessons learned in the kitchen of his grandmother. Bernard is now Chef de Cuisine at Emeril's Orlando, where his robust New Orleans food continues to draws legions of fans.

INGREDIENTS

2 tablespoons vegetable oil

1 smoked ham hock (about 4 ounces)

6 ounces thick slab bacon
(about 5 slices), chopped

1/2 cup chopped onion

1 tablespoon chopped garlic

1 (12-ounce) bottle Abita Amber

Tabasco sauce, salt, freshly ground black pepper
and crushed red pepper, to taste

16 cups loosely packed and washed greens,
such as kale, collards, mustard or beet

DIRECTIONS

Heat the oil in a large, heavy pot or Dutch oven over medium-low heat. Add the ham hock and bacon; cook, stirring, until the bacon begins to render some of the fat. Add the onion and garlic; cook, stirring, until the onions are soft, about 5 minutes. Stir in the beer. Season with Tabasco sauce, salt, black pepper and crushed red pepper. Bring to a boil.

Stir in the greens, a large handful at a time. When all greens have been added, reduce the heat to simmering, cover and cook until greens are very tender, about 15 minutes. Taste and adjust seasoning before serving.

BAKED BEANS
ABITA ROOT BEER STYLE

CHEF JOHN FOLSE · GONZALES, LOUISIANA

6 SERVINGS | *suggested pairing:* AMBER, JOCKAMO *or* TURBODOG · *made with* ROOT BEER

INGREDIENTS

1 pound bacon, diced
1 large onion, diced
6 ounces Abita Root Beer (3/4 cup)
2 (12-ounce) cans baked beans
1/4 cup barbecue sauce
1/2 teaspoon dry mustard

DIRECTIONS

Cook bacon in a saucepan over medium heat. Transfer bacon to paper towels to drain. Discard all but 2 tablespoons bacon drippings. Add onions and cook, stirring, for 3 to 5 minutes, or until translucent. Return bacon to pan. Add root beer, baked beans, barbecue sauce and dry mustard; mix well. Bring to a rolling boil. Reduce heat to a simmer. Cook 30 minutes, stirring occasionally. Serve hot.

WARM POTATO SALAD
WITH ABITA AMBER DRESSING

MARCELLE BIENVENU · ST. MARTINVILLE, LOUISIANA

6 SERVINGS

suggested pairing: AMBER, PECAN HARVEST *or* GOLDEN · *made with* AMBER

INGREDIENTS

2-1/2 pounds red potatoes, peeled if desired

4 hard-cooked eggs, peeled and coarsely chopped

1/4 cup minced fresh flat-leaf parsley

2 tablespoons minced green onions

Salt, freshly ground black pepper and cayenne pepper, to taste

6 tablespoons olive oil, divided

1/2 cup finely chopped sweet onions

3/4 cup Abita Amber

3 tablespoons cider vinegar

Pinch or two granulated sugar

1 tablespoon Creole mustard

Hot sauce, to taste

DIRECTIONS

Cook the potatoes in lightly salted boiling water until tender. Drain potatoes and let cool slightly. When cool enough to handle, coarsely chop the potatoes and put them in a large salad bowl. Add the eggs, parsley and green onions. Season with salt, black pepper and cayenne. Gently toss to mix. Heat 2 tablespoons of the olive oil in a skillet over medium heat. Add the onions and cook, stirring, until soft, 3 to 4 minutes. Add the beer, vinegar and sugar, Bring to a gentle boil. Cook for about 5 minutes.

Remove from the heat and transfer the mixture to a food processor or electric blender. Add the mustard. With the motor running, add the remaining 4 tablespoons olive oil through the feed tube or hole in lid. Season with hot sauce.

Drizzle the dressing over the potato mixture and toss gently to coat evenly.

TEMPURA FRIED VEGETABLES

MARCELLE BIENVENU · ST. MARTINVILLE, LOUISIANA

6-8 SERVINGS | *suggested pairing:* GOLDEN, RESTORATION ALE *or* AMBER · *made with* AMBER

INGREDIENTS

1/2 cup all-purpose flour

1/2 cup cornstarch

1 teaspoon baking soda

1 teaspoon baking powder

1/2 teaspoon salt

1 egg

2/3 cup Abita Amber

Vegetables of choice

Vegetable oil, for deep-frying

Creole or Cajun seasoning, to taste

Dipping sauce of choice

NOTE: The basic tempura batter also can be used for shrimp or chunks of chicken.

DIRECTIONS

For a basic tempura batter, sift the flour, cornstarch, baking soda, baking powder and salt into a mixing bowl. Whisk the egg with the beer. When the foam subsides, add the beer mixture to the flour mixture and stir until just mixed. The batter will be slightly lumpy.

Dip trimmed green beans, asparagus, okra and broccoli or cauliflower florets in the tempura batter and deep-fry in hot oil until golden brown. Drain on paper towels. Sprinkle with your favorite Creole or Cajun seasoning. Serve warm with your favorite dipping sauce.

ABITA BEER–BRAISED GREENS

CHEF DARIN NESBIT · DICKIE BRENNAN'S PALACE CAFÉ, NEW ORLEANS, LOUISIANA

12 SERVINGS | *suggested pairing:* RESTORATION ALE, JOCKAMO *or* AMBER · *made with* AMBER

The Palace Café has been serving award-winning contemporary Creole cuisine to locals and tourists alike since 1991 in the grand historic Werlein music building. Food & Wine, The New York Times and Wine Spectator are just a few of the publications that have recognized the outstanding food and great ambiance.

This is a traditional New Year's Day dish, which features 10 different types of greens, including cabbage for wealth in the New Year. According to legend, you'll meet/make a new friend for each type of green served.

INGREDIENTS

1 bunch each mustard greens, collard greens, turnip greens, watercress, beet tops, carrot tops, spinach, kale, cabbage and Swiss chard

1/4 cup olive oil

3 cups chopped onions

1/4 cup minced garlic

1 pound smoked sausage, cut crosswise into 1/4-inch slices

1 pound smoked tasso, finely chopped

1/2 pound smoked ham hocks

1 cup chopped pickled pork

2 quarts chicken stock

2 (12-ounce) bottles Abita Amber

1 cup cane vinegar

1/4 cup Steen's molasses

1 teaspoon chopped fresh thyme

1 tablespoon filé powder

Salt, black pepper, cayenne pepper and hot sauce, to taste

DIRECTIONS

Rinse all the greens several times under cool running water to remove soil and grit. (Some folks in South Louisiana use their washing machine on rinse cycle!) Remove and discard the large center stems. Coarsely chop the greens and set aside.

Heat the olive oil in a large, heavy pot or Dutch oven over medium heat. Add the onions, garlic, smoked sausage, tasso, ham hocks and pickled pork. Cook, stirring, until the vegetables are soft and the meat is lightly browned, 8 to 10 minutes.

Add the greens, stock, beer, cane vinegar and molasses. Bring the mixture to a rolling boil, then reduce heat and simmer, stirring occasionally, for 2 hours.

Remove the ham hocks and pick the meat off the bone. Return the meat to the pot along with the thyme and filé powder. Season with salt, pepper, cayenne and hot sauce. Serve hot.

TURBODOG BRAISED CABBAGE

EMERIL LAGASSE · EMERIL'S FOOD OF LOVE PRODUCTIONS (© 2007), NEW ORLEANS, LA

6-8 SERVINGS · *suggested pairing:* TURBODOG, FALL FEST *or* AMBER · *made with* TURBODOG

INGREDIENTS

1/2 pound bacon, chopped

2 cups thinly sliced onions

Freshly ground black pepper, to taste

1/4 cup Creole mustard

1/2 head white cabbage (about 1-1/2 pounds), shredded or thinly sliced

Salt, to taste

2 teaspoons chopped garlic

1 (12-ounce) bottle Abita Turbodog

1/4 cup heavy cream

DIRECTIONS

Put the bacon in a large saucepan over medium heat and render until crispy. Add the onions and season with pepper. Cook, stirring, until the onions are soft, about 4 minutes.

Add the mustard and cabbage. Season with salt and pepper. Cook, stirring, for 3 minutes. Add the garlic and beer. Cover and cook for 20 minutes, stirring occasionally.

Add the cream and stir to mix. Cook, covered, for 10 minutes. Serve warm.

IDEAS FOR VEGETABLES

MARCELLE BIENVENU · ST. MARTINVILLE, LOUISIANA

12 SERVINGS	*suggested pairing:* AMBER, WHEAT *or* GOLDEN · *made with* LIGHT

Boil vegetables such as leeks, Brussels sprouts, asparagus and green beans in your favorite Abita beer! Simply use beer rather than water or stock. Bring the beer to a gentle boil in a saucepan, drop in the vegetables and cook until just tender. Drain and serve.

The vegetables can be served as you would any side dish. Or, serve them for hors d'oeuvres with your favorite dipping sauce. Here are some suggested dipping sauces:

INGREDIENTS

LIME-BUTTER SAUCE – *Makes about 2/3 cup*

2 tablespoons minced shallots

1 teaspoon grated lime peel

1/4 cup fresh lime juice

1/4 cup Abita Light

1 tablespoon cold water

1 stick (1/2 cup) cold unsalted butter, cut into bits

White pepper and salt, to taste

CURRY DIP – *Makes about 1 cup*

1 cup mayonnaise

1 teaspoon curry powder

1 teaspoon prepared horseradish

1 teaspoon tarragon vinegar

1 tablespoon minced onion

1/4 teaspoon hot sauce

Salt and freshly ground black pepper, to taste

LIME-BUTTER SAUCE

Cook the shallots, lime peel, lime juice and beer in a small, heavy, stainless-steel or enameled saucepan over medium heat until the liquid is reduced to about 2 tablespoons. Remove the pan from the heat and add the cold water. Reduce the heat to low and whisk in the butter, one piece at a time, lifting the pan from the heat occasionally to cool the mixture. The mixture should be the consistency of Hollandaise sauce. Whisk in the white pepper and salt. Serve immediately.

> NOTE: The Lime-Butter Sauce is also great to pour over grilled fish or chicken.

CURRY DIP

Combine mayonnaise, curry powder, horseradish, vinegar, onion, hot sauce, salt and pepper in a small mixing bowl; whisk to blend well. Store in the refrigerator in an airtight container for up to three days.

DESSERTS

CAKES, ICE CREAMS & OTHER SWEET TREATS

COOKING LOUISIANA TRUE

CHAPTER
No. 5

LOUISIANA TRUE BEERAMISU

Jeff Cuppie · Mandeville, Louisiana

| 12 SERVINGS | *suggested pairing:* PURPLE HAZE, AMBER *or* GOLDEN · *made with* PURPLE HAZE |

INGREDIENTS

1 cup heavy cream

8 ounces mascarpone cheese (see note)

3/4 cup confectioners' sugar

1/4 cup seedless raspberry jam

2 tablespoons pure vanilla extract

1 (12-ounce) bottle Abita Purple Haze

1/2 cup brewed coffee,
the stronger the better (see note)

1 (7-ounce) package ladyfinger cookies (or one
12-ounce box vanilla wafers)

DIRECTIONS

Whip the heavy cream on high speed of electric mixer until stiff and thick. Combine the mascarpone, confectioners' sugar, raspberry jam and vanilla in a large bowl; mix well. Fold in the whipped cream. Set aside.

Pour half of the beer into a shallow bowl. (Drink the rest of the beer.) Stir in the brewed coffee. Dip the ladyfinger cookies (or vanilla wafers) into the beer-coffee mixture. Don't let them get soggy. Just put them in for a second, then take them out immediately. Arrange the dipped cookies in a single layer in a glass serving dish. (The smaller the dish, the higher or thicker the Beeramisu will be.) Spread a 1/2-inch layer of the mascarpone mixture on top of the layer of cookies. Repeat layers until all mascarpone mixture and cookies are used. Cover and refrigerate for at least 2 hours before serving.

NOTE: Mascarpone cheese is sometimes hard to find. You can substitute ricotta cheese, but be sure to blend it until it is a smooth consistency. To keep "Louisiana True," use chicory coffee and brew it extremely strong. You can substitute other Abita beers to change it up a bit. Strawberry Harvest Lager works well with strawberry jelly instead of raspberry jam. Turbodog would be great in the winter, or Pecan Harvest Ale in the fall.

TURBODOG ICE CREAM

MARCELLE BIENVENU · ST. MARTINVILLE, LOUISIANA

1 QUART

suggested pairing: TURBODOG, ANDYGATOR *or* BOCK · *made with* TURBODOG

INGREDIENTS

1 (12-ounce) bottle Abita Turbodog

2 cups heavy cream

2 cups whole milk

3/4 cup natural cane turbinado sugar
(brand name Sugar in the Raw)

1 tablespoon pure vanilla extract

6 egg yolks

DIRECTIONS

Pour the Turbodog into a small, heavy saucepan over medium heat. Bring to a gentle boil and reduce by half. Remove from the heat and let cool completely.

Combine the cream, milk, sugar and vanilla in a medium, heavy, non-reactive saucepan over medium heat and cook, stirring until the sugar dissolves and the mixture is hot. DO NOT BOIL. Remove from the heat.

Whisk the egg yolks in a bowl. Slowly add one cup of the cream mixture to the yolks, whisking constantly until smooth. Slowly pour the yolk mixture back into the cream, whisking constantly. Place the saucepan back on medium heat. Cook, stirring constantly, until the mixture thickens enough to coat the back of a spoon, 6 to 8 minutes. DO NOT BOIL.

Pour the mixture through a fine strainer into a clean bowl. Cover with plastic wrap, pressing down against the surface to keep a skin from forming. Refrigerate for at least 2 hours.

Remove from the refrigerator and add the Turbodog reduction, whisking to blend. Pour the mixture into an ice cream machine and freeze according to manufacturer's directions. Transfer to an airtight container and store in the freezer until ready to serve.

ABITA PURPLE HAZE BARS

CHEF HOLLY GOETTING · CHARLEY G'S, NEW ORLEANS, LOUISIANA

9 BARS

suggested pairing: PURPLE HAZE, GOLDEN *or* STRAWBERRY HARVEST
made with PURPLE HAZE

INGREDIENTS

CRUST
1-1/4 cups graham cracker crumbs
1/4 cup granulated sugar
4 tablespoons unsalted butter, melted

CUSTARD FILLING
1/4 cup granulated sugar
3 tablespoons cornstarch
1 (12-ounce) can evaporated milk
6 ounces (3/4 cup) Abita Purple Haze
4 egg yolks
1 teaspoon almond extract
1 teaspoon pure vanilla extract
2 cups fresh raspberries
2 cups fresh blackberries
1/2 cup confectioners' sugar

CRUST

Preheat the oven to 350 degrees. Combine the graham cracker crumbs, sugar and butter in a mixing bowl; stir to mix well. Press the mixture into the bottom and up the sides of a 9-inch square baking pan. (Tip: Use another 9-inch square baking pan to press the mixture tightly into the pan and slightly up the sides. Remove second pan.) Bake in 350-degree oven until lightly browned and set, about 8 minutes. Remove from oven and set aside to cool completely. Turn off the oven.

CUSTARD FILLING

Combine the sugar and cornstarch in a stainless-steel bowl; stir to blend. Add the evaporated milk, beer, egg yolks, almond extract and vanilla. Whisk to blend. Set the bowl over a pot of just-simmering water (or put the mixture in the top of a double boiler over just-simmering water) and cook, stirring constantly, until the mixture thickens enough to coat the back of a spoon, 8 to 10 minutes.

Pour the custard into the cooled graham cracker crumb crust. Pat the berries dry with a paper towel and arrange berries over the top of the custard. Refrigerate until the custard sets, at least 3 hours.

Cut into 9 bars. Sprinkle with confectioners' sugar before serving.

ABITA GOLDEN BANANAS

MILES MAYEUX · BATON ROUGE, LOUISIANA

2-4 SERVINGS	*suggested pairing:* STRAWBERRY HARVEST, CHRISTMAS ALE *or* GOLDEN *made with* GOLDEN

Use these bananas as a topping for your favorite ice cream, cheesecake or sponge cake.

INGREDIENTS

1 tablespoon unsalted butter
1 heaping tablespoon light brown sugar
1/3 cup Abita Golden
2 ripe bananas

DIRECTIONS

Melt the butter in a skillet over medium-low heat. Add the brown sugar and stir to dissolve. Slowly add the beer. Simmer, stirring, until the sauce thickens slightly.

Peel the bananas. Cut them in half crosswise, then slice lengthwise. Add the banana pieces to sauce and cook about 2 minutes on each side. Serve warm.

PURPLE HAZE SORBET

CHEF DON WILKINSON · DICKIE BRENNAN'S BOURBON HOUSE, NEW ORLEANS, LOUISIANA

1.5 GALLONS	*suggested pairing:* PURPLE HAZE, STRAWBERRY HARVEST *or* GOLDEN *made with* PURPLE HAZE

INGREDIENTS

2 quarts granulated sugar

2 quarts water

2 quarts fresh raspberries

2 quarts Abita Purple Haze

DIRECTIONS

Combine sugar and water in a large pot; bring mixture to a boil; stir until sugar is dissolved. This is a simple syrup. Remove from heat and let cool.

Add raspberries to cooled syrup and blend (using a food processor, blender or mixer). You probably will need to do this in batches. Strain the blended mixture to remove seeds. Discard seeds.

Transfer strained mixture to a freezable container. Stir in the beer; mix well. Freeze mixture overnight or until firm.

ROOT BEER FLOAT
WITH PIROUETTE COOKIES

OLIVE GILTHORPE & MAGGIE MAE BALLARD · NEW ORLEANS, LOUISIANA

| 4 SERVINGS | *made with* ROOT BEER |

It's best to use tall, pre-chilled (put them in the freezer for a couple of hours) glasses or mugs for the best results. The pirouette cookies take a little time to prepare, but you can certainly substitute store-bought ones if you like.

INGREDIENTS

4 to 5 (12-ounce) bottles cold Abita Root Beer
(amount depends on size of glasses)
4 to 8 scoops vanilla ice cream
(amount depends on size of glasses)
Whipped cream, for garnish
1/4 cup toasted shredded coconut, for garnish
Pirouette Cookies, for garnish

PIROUETTE COOKIES - *Makes 25 to 30 cookies*
2 tablespoons confectioners' sugar
2 tablespoons chopped pecans
1/3 cup granulated sugar
1/3 cup all-purpose flour
1/4 teaspoon salt
3 egg whites, lightly beaten
1 tablespoon light corn syrup
1/4 cup unsalted butter, softened
1/2 teaspoon pure vanilla extract

DIRECTIONS

Pour the root beer to fill each glass about half full. Add one or two scoops of ice cream. Drizzle a small amount of root beer on top of the ice cream. This will cause a foam to form. Continue drizzling until the glass is almost full. Top each glass with a dollop of whipped cream. Sprinkle each serving with a tablespoon of the shredded coconut. Insert 1 to 2 Pirouette Cookies in the float and serve immediately.

PIROUETTE COOKIES
Preheat the oven to 425 degrees. Spray two baking sheets with vegetable cooking spray.

Combine the confectioners' sugar and pecans in a food processor and pulse several times until the mixture is very fine. Add the granulated sugar, flour and salt, and process until well mixed. Add the egg whites, corn syrup, butter and vanilla and process until a dough forms.

Drop the dough by rounded teaspoonfuls (about 2-1/2 inches apart) onto the prepared baking sheets. Bake in 425-degree oven until the edges of the cookies are golden, about 5 minutes. Remove from the oven and place the baking sheets on wire racks.

With a spatula, place each cookie on a clean kitchen towel (not terrycloth) and carefully roll the warm cookie securely around the handle of a wooden spoon or dowel, pressing gently but firmly as you roll. Carefully slide the cookie off the spoon handle and place on wire rack to cool. Repeat the process with the remaining cookies. Try to work quickly as the cookies must be warm for the rolling procedure. If they cool, they will not roll.

PECAN SPICE BEER CAKE
WITH BROWN BUTTER PECAN GLAZE

CHEF PAUL CONWAY · GLORIOSA CATERING, ATLANTA, GEORGIA

1 CAKE	*suggested pairing:* AMBER, CHRISTMAS ALE *or* PECAN HARVEST
	made with PECAN HARVEST

INGREDIENTS

2 cups light brown sugar

2 sticks (1 cup) butter, softened

2 eggs

3 cups all-purpose flour

1 teaspoon ground cinnamon

1 teaspoon ground allspice

1/2 teaspoon freshly grated nutmeg

2 teaspoons baking powder

1 cup golden raisins

1 cup chopped pecans

1 Granny Smith apple, peeled and grated

1 teaspoon pure vanilla extract

1 (12-ounce) bottle Abita Pecan
Harvest Ale, divided

BROWN BUTTER PECAN GLAZE

1 stick (1/2 cup) butter

1 cup chopped pecans

2 tablespoons Abita Pecan Harvest Ale

2 cups confectioners' sugar

DIRECTIONS

Preheat the oven to 325 degrees. Mix the brown sugar with the butter in a large mixing bowl until light and fluffy. Add the eggs, one at a time, beating well after each addition. Sift the flour, cinnamon, allspice, nutmeg and baking powder into another mixing bowl. Combine the raisins, pecans and apple in another bowl.

Stir one-third of the flour mixture into the brown sugar mixture. Add the vanilla and half of the beer. Gently stir in another one-third of the flour mixture and the remaining beer. Combine the remaining one-third of the flour mixture with the raisin-pecan-apple mixture; toss to mix and coat fruit and nuts. Add to the batter and mix well.

Pour batter into prepared pan and bake in 325-degree oven until a cake tester comes out clean, about 1 hour. Remove the cake from the oven and let cool completely.

While cake is cooling, prepare Brown Butter Pecan Glaze. Remove the cake from the pan and put on a cake platter or stand. Spoon the glaze over the cooled cake.

BROWN BUTTER PECAN GLAZE

Melt the butter in a small saucepan over medium heat. Add the pecans; stir constantly over medium heat to toast the pecans and allow the butter to brown slowly, 3 to 5 minutes.

Remove from the heat and pour the mixture into a stainless-steel mixing bowl to cool completely. When cool, add the beer and confectioners' sugar; stir by hand or with an electric mixer until well blended.

INDEX

A

Abbey Ale
    photo, 32
    about, 47
    suggested pairing, 109, 111, 130, 140
Abita Amber Soup, 65-66
Abita Beer
    history, 11
    brewing, 22-29
    serving, 34-35
    enjoying, 36-39
Abita Brew Pub
    history, 11
    recipe, 79
Abita Dinner Series, 49
Abita Flagship Brews, 40-43
Abita Select
    about, 48
    recipe, 67
Abita Springs
    history of Abita Beer, 11
    photo, 13
    history of town, 22-24
Aging, 29
Alligator, 58
Amber
    photo, 10, 32, 65, 89
    history, 11
    about, 40
    cooking with beer, 53
    recipe ingredient, 57, 61, 62-63, 66, 69, 78, 79, 81-82,
        86, 90-91, 93-95, 100-101, 107, 109, 110, 116-117, 121,
        127, 129, 138, 144, 147-149
    suggested pairing, 57, 61, 66-67, 69, 72, 78-79, 83, 86,
        90, 93, 97, 99-100, 102-103, 107, 111, 113, 116-117,
        119, 121-123, 127, 129, 133, 136-138, 140, 144-145,
        147-151, 155, 164
American Brewery Company, 16

American Society of Brewing Chemists, 36
Andouille, 107, 110
Andrew Jackson, 19, 21
Andygator
    aging, 29
    photo, 32
    about, 47
    suggested pairing, 78, 123, 157

B

Bacco Crab Cakes, 97-98
Ballard, Maggie Mae, 163
Banana, 159
Barbecued Alligator Legs, 58
Barbecued Oysters, 100-101
Barley
    brewing, 22, 28
    about, 23-24
Bayona Restaurant, 103
Bayou Restaurant, 61
Beans, 145, 148, 151
Beef
    suggested pairing, 44
    cooking with beer, 53
    recipes, 115-117, 122-123, 130-131, 137
Beer-B-Q Glaze, 92-95
Beer-Battered Tempura Soft-Shell Crabs, 62-64
Beer Bitterness, 39
Beer Color, 38
Beer Clean, 34
Beer Flavor Wheel, 36-37
Beer Gardens of New Orleans, 16-17
Beer Hues In Lovibond Units, 38-39
Beer Stein, 34
Beeramisu, 155
Bienvenu, Marcelle
    about, 5, 7
    recipes, 86, 129, 136, 147-148, 151, 157

Biscuits, 75, 90-91
Bitter
    about, 28
    tasting test, 36
    cooking with beer, 53
Bitterness Comparison Chart, 39
Blackened Redfish, 100-101
Blossman, David, 3, 11
Bock
    about, 44
    suggested pairing, 62, 115, 125, 157
    recipe ingredient, 129
Boil, 26, 28
Bottling, 29
Bourbon House, 109, 113, 161
Bratwurst, 119
Bread
    and beer history, 22, 47
    yeast and beer, 26
    recipes, 73, 81
Brennan, Dickie 149, 161
Brewmaster, 22, 28
Burns, Tom, 99

C

Cabbage
    braised, 100-101
    and tasso hash, 139
Café Adelaide, 90
Caffeine
    and Abita Root Beer, 11, 49
Cane Syrup, 109, 140-141
Caramel, 40, 44, 47
Carbonation
    brewing, 29
    enjoying, 31
    glassware, 35
Carmouche, Bernard, 144

Castillo, Ignacio, 99
Ceviche Beer Shots, 57
Chalice, 35
Charley G's Restaurant, 62, 77, 158
Chicken
    cooking with beer, 53
    chicken stock, 66, 72, 99, 109, 111, 125, 130, 136,
        138, 149
    recipe ingredient, 107, 121, 125, 127, 138
Chocolate Malt, 24, 25
Choctaw Indian, 22
Chorizo, 125
Christmas Ale
    aging, 29
    pairing, 31
    about, 45
    suggested pairing, 83, 117, 136-137, 159, 164
Cilantro Rice, 129
Clarified Butter, 86
CO_2 (Carbon Dioxide), 29
Cochon Restaurant, 69, 110
Coffee, 155
Collards, 144
Collier, Greg, 58, 100
Commander's Palace
    and Marcelle Bienvenu, 7
    recipe, 111
Complement, 31
Connaughton, Jay, 133
Contrast, 31
Conway, Paul, 57, 164
Crabfingers, 59, 79
Crabmeat
    cooking with beer, 53
    recipes, 78, 97
Crawfish (or Crayfish)
    suggested pairing, 40, 43, 47
    recipes, 78, 103, 107

Cuppie, Jeff, 155
Cut, 31
Cuvée, 139

D

Dakota Restaurant, 78
Delta Grill, 99
Dickie Brennan, see Brennan, Dickie
The Dixie Brewing Company, 21
Dore, Eula Mae, 7

E

Emeril, see Lagasse, Emeril
Enzymes, 24, 28
European Brewery Convention, 36

F

Fabacher, Lawrence, 21
Fall Fest
    about, 45
    suggested pairing, 58, 72, 93, 109-110, 113, 119,
        139, 150
Falstaff Brewery, 14, 20-21
Fermentation, 22, 26, 29
Filtration, 29, 42
Flute Glass, 35
Folse, John, 145

G

Galatoire's, 67, 86
Garcia, Adolfo, 125, 130
Gaxholli, Julian, 61
Gilthorpe, Olive, 163
Glassware, 34-35
Gloriosa Catering, 57, 164
Goblet, 35, 42, 44-45, 47
Goetting, Holly, 62, 77, 158
Golden

history, 11
aging, 29
suggested pairing, 59, 62, 69, 79, 99, 107, 125, 147-148,
    151, 155, 158-159, 161
photo, 33
about, 43
recipe ingredient, 57, 59, 75, 86, 99, 123, 125, 129, 159
Grain, 24, 28,
Grist, 28
Gumbo, 107

H

Harris, Megan, 107
Harvest Brews, 46
Hells Dopple Bock, 47
Henriques, 24
Hermecz, Denis, 82
Home-brewing, 11
Hooks, Matt, 5
Hops (Hoppy)
    history, 16
    ingredients, 22, 24
    photo, 25
    brewing, 28-29
    flavor, 36
    bitterness, 39
House of Blues Foundation Room, 140
Hurricane Katrina, 3, 13, 41
Hushpuppies, 82

I

Iacovone, Bob, 139
IBU, see International Bitterness Units
Ice Cream, 157
India Pale Ale, 41, 48
International Bitterness Units, 39-47

J

Jackson Brewing Company, 18-19, 21
Jackson Square, 19, 21
Jacques-Imo's, 123
James Beard Foundation, 111
Jax Beer, 18-19, 21
Jochum, Cherry, 73
Jockamo I. P. A.
   history, 11
   hops and, 26, 29
   photo, 32
   about, 41
   cooking with beer, 53
   suggested pairing, 58, 66, 107, 109, 110, 115-116,
      122, 127, 139, 140, 144-145, 149
   recipe ingredient, 133, 140
Juban's Restaurant, 59, 71

K

K-Paul's Restaurant
   and Marcelle Bienvenu, 7
   recipes, 83, 137
Kling, Dusty, 119
Kringlie, Kim, 78
Kyles, Erin, 66

L

Lagasse, Emeril, 7, 93, 144, 150
Lager
   history, 15
   brewing, 24
   styles, 40-47
   cooking with beer, 53
Landry, Brian, 67, 86
Lauter Tun, 28
Leonardi, Jacques, 123

Light

Light
   suggested pairing, 67, 93
   recipe ingredient, 137
Link, Donald, 69, 110
Lombardo, Patrice, 116
Louis XVI Restaurant, 115
Lovibond Units, 38-39

M

Magic Seasoning Blends, 83
Malts, 24-25
Mardi Gras Indians, 41
Martin, Gus, 138
Mash, 28
Master Brewers Association, 36
Mayeux, Miles, 159
McDonner, Terry, 59, 71
McPhail, Tory, 111
Meilgaard, Dr. Morten, 36
The Merz Brewery, 15
Merz, George, 15
Microbrewery, 11
Montero, Chris, 97
Morrow, William, 7
Mouthfeel, 36
Mussels
   cooking with beer, 53
   recipe, 61

N

National Brewing Company, 21
Nesbit, Darin, 109, 113, 149
New Orleans Barbecue Shrimp Shortcakes, 89-91
Nuts
   beer flavor, 11
   suggested pairing, 45-46, 164

O

Octoberfest (Oktoberfest), 45
Olfactory, 36
Olivard, Chad, 75, 117
Oxtails, 130-131
Oysters, 67, 100-101

P

Pairing, 31
Palace Café, 149
Palate, 31
Pan-Roasted Chicken, 138
Pasta, 40, 43, 45
Pecan Harvest Ale
    about, 46
    suggested pairing, 86, 130, 138, 147, 155, 164
Pecan Meuniere, 86- 88
Pecans
    about Pecan Harvest Ale, 46
    suggested pairing, 71
    recipe, 86, 163-164
Pie Crust, 140-141
Pilsner, 35, 40-45
Pint Glass, 34
Pirouette Cookies, 163
Pizza, 132-135
Pomodori, 59
Ponzu Dipping Sauce, 62-63
Pork Meat Pies, 140-141
Preservatives, 15
Process
    of making beer, 22-29
Prudhomme, Paul, 83, 99, 137
Purple Haze
    history, 11
    photo, 32
    about, 42

    cooking with beer, 53
    suggested pairing, 71, 77, 83, 155, 158, 161
    recipe ingredient, 71, 83, 155, 158, 161

R

Rabbit, 136
Raisin-pecan-apple, 164
Raisins, 164
Raspberry
    in Purple Haze, 11 , 42, 71, 155
Red Ale
    about, 29, 44
    suggested pairing, 100
Red Fish Grill, 58, 100
Restoration Pale Ale
    history, 11
    photo, 13
    about, 26, 41
    cooking with beer, 53
    suggested pairing, 59, 61, 77-78, 97, 99, 113, 121, 129,
        133, 138, 144, 148-149
Rice Pilaf, 86-87
Riomar, 125, 130
Robinson, Keith, 57
Root Beer
    history, 11
    photo, 33
    about, 48
    recipe ingredient, 139, 145, 163
    cooking with beer, 53
Roux, 67, 78, 107, 111, 121, 136
Royal Sonesta Hotel, 16

S

Saison, 67
Salad
    cooking with beer, 31, 53
    recipe, 69, 71, 77, 113, 147

Salmon, 57

Sauerkraut, 119

Sausage, 107, 110, 125, 149

Sautéed Snapper, 86-88

Scallops, 57

Sciortino, Gia, 72

Seafood Beignets, 78

Seasonal Brews, 44-45

Select
   history, 11
   about, 49
   recipe ingredient, 67

Select Dinners, 49

Shepherd's Pie, 137

Shrimp
   cooking with beer, 53, 57, 77-78, 89-91, 93-95, 99,
      102-103, 107

Sichel, Michael, 127

Slow Food, 122

Smoked Cheddar Grits, 93, 95

Snapper, 86- 88

Snifter, 35

Soft-shell crabs, 62-64

Sorbet, 161

Soup
   cooking with beer, 53, 65-67, 72

Sparge, Sparging, 28

Spectrophotometer, 38

Spicer, Susan, 103

Starch, 24

Stein, 34

Strawberry, 77

Strawberry Harvest Lager
   history, 11
   about, 46
   cooking with beer, 53
   suggested pairing, 77, 155, 158-159, 161
   recipe ingredient, 77

Stryjewski, Stephen, 69, 110

Sullivan, Tom, 99

Sunlight, 34

Sweetness
   hops and, 24, 28

Swizzle Stick Bar, 90

T

Tammany Trace, 79

Tankard, 34

Tannin, 28

Tap
   photo, 26-27
   pouring beer, 34

The Tasting Test, 36

Tempura, 62-64, 148,

The Three C's, 31

Tivoli Gardens, 16-17

Tony Chachere's, 66, 127

Tooker, Poppy, 121-122

Top-fermented, 47

Trace, Danny, 90

Tritium, 22

Tujague, Kathy, 81, 102

Tulip Glass, 35

Turbodog
   history, 11
   photo, 32
   about, 38, 42
   recipe ingredient, 58, 61, 72, 75, 97-98, 102, 115, 119,
      122-123, 130-136, 150, 157
   cooking with beer, 31, 53
   suggested pairing, 58, 61-62, 66, 72, 79, 97, 102,
      110-111, 115-117, 119, 121-123, 127, 130, 136-137, 139,
      145, 150, 157

Turbodog Creole Mustard Aioli, 97-98

U

Umami, 36

V

Valentine Merz, 21

W

Wheat
  about, 45
  recipe ingredient, 103
  suggested pairing, 67, 71, 90, 103, 125, 129, 151
Wilkinson, Don, 161
Winowich, Nathan, 140
Wit Beer, 48
Wort, 20, 28-29

Y

Yeast, 22, 26, 28-29
  recipe ingredient, 73

TABLE OF EQUIVALENTS & FOOD HANDLING

COOKING MEASUREMENT EQUIVALENTS

1 tablespoon (tbsp) =	3 teaspoons (tsp)
1/16 cup (c) =	1 tablespoon
1/8 cup =	2 tablespoons
1/6 cup =	2 tablespoons + 2 teaspoons
1/4 cup =	4 tablespoons
1/3 cup =	5 tablespoons + 1 teaspoon
3/8 cup =	6 tablespoons
1/2 cup =	8 tablespoons
2/3 cup =	10 tablespoons + 2 teaspoons
3/4 cup =	12 tablespoons
1 cup =	48 teaspoons
1 cup =	16 tablespoons
8 fluid ounces (fl oz) =	1 cup
1 pint (pt) =	2 cups
1 quart (qt) =	2 pints
4 cups =	1 quart
1 gallon (gal) =	4 quarts
16 ounces (oz) =	1 pound (lb)
1 milliliter (ml) =	1 cubic centimeter (cc)
1 inch (in) =	2.54 centimeters (cm)

SAFE MINIMUM INTERNAL TEMPERATURES

PRODUCT	TYPE	TEMP
Beef & Veal	Ground	160ºF
	Steak & roasts medium	160ºF
	Steak & roasts medium rare	145ºF
Chicken & Turkey	Breasts	165ºF
	Ground, stuffing, and casseroles	165ºF
	Whole bird, legs, thighs, and wings	165ºF
Eggs	Any type	160ºF
Fish & Shellfish	Any type	145ºF
Lamb	Ground	160ºF
	Steak and roasts medium	160ºF
	Steaks and roasts medium rare	145ºF
Leftovers	Any type	165ºF
Pork	Chops, fresh (raw) ham ground, ribs, and roasts	160ºF
	Fully cooked ham (to reheat)	140ºF